**The Hidden Language
of Your Handwriting**

Also by David Lewis
in Pan Books

How to Be a Gifted Parent
The Secret Language of Your Child

James Greene MA and David Lewis

The Hidden Language of Your Handwriting

The remarkable new science of
graphonomy and what it reveals about
personality, health and emotions

Pan Books London and Sydney

First published 1980 by Souvenir Press Ltd
This edition published 1982 by Pan Books Ltd,
Cavaye Place SW10 9PG
© James Greene and David Lewis 1980
ISBN 0 330 26695 0
Printed and bound in Great Britain by
Hazell Watson & Viney Ltd, Aylesbury, Bucks

'The Moving Finger writes; and, having writ,
Moves on: nor all thy Piety nor Wit
Shall lure it back to cancel half a Line,
Nor all your Tears wash out a Word of it.'

Rubaiyat of Omar Khayyám

Contents

Introduction

An interest in the inner meaning of handwriting is as ancient as the art of writing itself. As long ago as AD 1000 Chinese scholars tried to probe personality through script analysis. Greek and Roman philosophers believed writing might be used to reveal aspects of character and abilities. During the 17th century an Italian, Dr. Baldi, attempted a systematic approach to analysis which was taken further at the start of the 19th century by the Swiss pastor Lavater.

But it was not until 1875, with the publication of a serious book on the subject by the Frenchman Abbé Jean-Hippolyte Michon, that the foundations of modern graphology were laid down. It was the Abbé who first coined that name – from the Greek words *graphein*, to write and *logos*, account – and set about assessing an individual's character from the signs in the handwriting.

The apparent simplicity of the Abbé's methods attracted a passionate but superficial interest during the decades that followed. For the Victorians it became part parlour game and part legitimate inquiry. However, the frivolity which surrounded graphology soon attracted fierce criticism from responsible scientists. They rightly pointed out that the methods used were highly suspect, the predictions unreliable and the procedures lacking in serious credibility.

Those who insisted that handwriting analysis offered a perfect means of assessing their fellow man were right in believing that it can, indeed, provide vital and accurate insights. But their approach was so unscientific as to make any such assessments little better than guesswork. They owed too much to intuition, surmise and chance. Not surprisingly they were often wide of the mark.

Rival systems of interpretation were developed in different countries but they were all created in much the same way. What the analysts would do was look at a sample of handwriting produced by some famous individual, a statesman, soldier or actress for instance. They would then extract various characteristics from the shape of letters and words, asserting that these indicated the special abilities which had made those writers famous – or notorious. Graphologists would then claim that these same characteristics, whenever found in an individual's writing, indicated similar personality traits or intellectual potential.

Given such a haphazard approach it was hardly surprising that graphologists were unable to agree among themselves about the meaning of particular handwriting characteristics or that they found it impossible to come to consistently reliable conclusions about individual writers.

Since those early days the process of analysis has been refined but it is only in the past few years that true scientific method has been brought to bear on the interpretation of handwriting. Using computers, advanced statistical procedures and a wide range of modern technology, researchers in such diverse fields as psychology and education, medicine and criminal detection, have now written a whole new chapter in the history of handwriting analysis.

We have coined the term *graphonomy* to distinguish between the modern approach and the old-fashioned techniques of graphology. In doing so we intend to draw a comparison between its methodical procedures and those of astronomy, a precise science which can make accurate predictions about the movements of stars and planets at enormous distances and over vast periods of time. By applying the laws of physics and mathematics to the mysterious regions of space one can not only state with certainty that certain events will occur, but also explain how, when, where and why they will take place. Graphonomy provides the same sort of fine precision when it comes to interpreting handwriting samples.

Graphology, on the other hand, is closer to astrology in its method and results. While astrologers, like graphologists, can make accurate predictions on occasions the results are frequently unreliable. The statements made by both tend to be often vague generalisations which may be no better than pure guess-work. Graphologists are often uncertain why particular characteristics of the script should be linked to a specific sort of personality and they are unable to agree among themselves about the real meaning of many such signs. They cannot say how internal changes in the writer's physical or emotional state are reflected in the way letters and words are formed. They are unable to state when changes in writing style indicate short-term difficulties rather than long-term problems. Because it has no scientifically supported laws behind the theory, graphology – like astrology – must frequently be imprecise and ambiguous in its conclusions.

In the hands of highly experienced practitioners, who have an intuitive understanding of human nature and possess deep psychological insights, both astrology and graphology can, it is true, come up with remarkably accurate predictions and assessments. But often these revelations are due more to the skill of those making the analysis rather than any intrinsic merits of the techniques they apparently use.

This brings us to another problem encountered by those who want to learn how to interpret handwriting. Because it demands much knowledge besides the actual procedures of analysis, and because these procedures tend to be confusingly complex in themselves, learning to use it successfully is a long and frustrating business.

Graphonomy, by comparison, is relatively quick to learn and absolutely straightforward to apply. It is reliable because the scientists who developed its procedures tended to work in areas, such as medical diagnosis, where error and ambiguity simply could not be tolerated. Its advantages over the earlier approach can easily be summarised.

*Its predictions are accurate.

*Its assessments are reliable.

*It can be applied easily, efficiently and confidently from the first.

*It can offer information in areas where considerable importance must be attached to the conclusions – for example when looking at any health problems or emotional difficulties the writer may be suffering.

*The procedures are straightforward and can be mastered with only a small amount of practice.

We believe that the techniques of graphonomy provide a vital new approach to a better understanding of ourselves and others. Whatever your professional or personal interests we are sure that you will find the methods of analysis described in this book not only fascinating but of great practical value. They will give you the opportunity to acquire insights and information which could not be obtained in any other way. They will probably tell you things about yourself you never knew and things about other people of which even they were completely unaware.

Chapter One

The New Science of Graphonomy

As an art, handwriting analysis was born into a world of gas lighting and horse-drawn carriages. As a science it has just come of age in the austere surroundings of the laboratory, consulting room and clinic. What was once a process based largely on hunch and intuition has been transformed into an exercise in refined, modern technology. A parlour game which entertained the Victorians has finally achieved the status of a respectable academic study. As a result of intensive research in Europe and America a whole new range of analytical procedures has been developed which are precise enough to satisfy the stringent standards of scientific inquiry; reliable enough to meet the needs of industry, education, medical diagnosis and psychological assessment; yet simple enough to be used by any intelligent individual with only a small amount of practice.

The name of this new approach to the fascinating business of handwriting analysis is *graphonomy*. The purpose of this book is to show you how you can learn and apply its principles, quickly, easily and effectively. To explain the wide range of important insights that can be gained, and to describe the practical ways in which a knowledge of scientifically based graphonomy could help to enhance your understanding of yourself and others.

HOW YOU CAN USE GRAPHONOMY

Experience has proved that this valuable technique can find a use in almost every area of life. At the end of this chapter we will be suggesting many specific ways in which you might put the procedures to work for you. Here we will simply outline some of the reasons why learning graphonomy could prove the most worthwhile investment in personal growth you have ever made.

It may be used to gain greater insights into your own personality, and needs. To explore the attitudes of your relatives and friends and to find out what sort of a relationship you might expect to enjoy with a particular writer in the role of employer, employee, friend, a marriage partner or a lover.

At a personal level, graphonomy gives you important insights into your own state of mental or physical health. It can provide a warning – well in advance of any other indications – that stress levels are now high and the time has come to ease off the pressure, to adopt a more relaxed approach to life. Or it may reveal that your lifestyle is too lacking in stimulation and that a change of routine is desired.

Parents will find handwriting analysis, based on these new procedures, a valuable method for discovering any emotional or educational problems faced by their children. Through the early detection of rising levels of stress, they will be able to provide the most effective help and advice. Handwriting is also a potent predictor of intellectual ability. It enables parents and teachers to spot the child who is an early or late developer and give them the most useful assistance.

At work, employers will find that an analysis of handwriting can often save them from making serious errors when hiring staff. It allows them to assess the applicant's personality, to assess his, or her, activity level – so discovering how much energy and enthusiasm is likely to be invested in the job – and to detect signs of emotional disturbance. It enables a prediction to be made about the writer's probable response to stress, indicates how they will react in a crisis and suggests their reaction to criticism.

All these and many more uses for graphonomy will be described in detail in the chapters which follow.

With such powerful techniques of assessment available to them through graphonomy, it is hardly surprising that an increasing number of organisations and individuals are using the new science in areas where there is no room for error. Many multi-national companies, for example, use its procedures to assess the suitability of job applicants at senior levels. A major London insurance brokerage determines the honesty of people applying for security bonding by means of handwriting analysis. Dr. Roda Wieser, one of Austria's leading criminologists, regards such interpretations as providing a major procedure for understanding the criminal mind. In America, Dr. Ulrich Sonnemann, formerly Professor of Clinical Psychology at the New School University in New York, found it an invaluable diagnostic aid for the early detection of mental illness; Dr. Richard Pearl, at New York's Mount Sinai Hospital, uses it to keep a check on the progress of his seriously ill patients, while Professor Philip Vernon of Calgary University, Alberta – one of the world's most eminent educational psychologists – has concluded that handwriting can provide a valuable index of the pattern of personality.

WHY GRAPHONOMY WORKS SO WELL

There are six major reasons why the scientific study of handwriting has made such a valuable contribution to our understanding of human potential.

1. The predictions are highly reliable. In medical diagnosis, for example, 90% accuracy has been achieved in some areas. Using nothing more than the patient's handwriting, many diseases have been correctly diagnosed long before they could have been detected by other medical procedures.
2. It will enable you to monitor important aspects of health and happiness on a day-to-day basis. What is more, such regular checks can be undertaken quickly, easily and accurately using equipment no more complicated than a sheet of paper and a fountain pen.
3. It provides insights into *why* people behave in certain ways, as well as revealing *how* they are most likely to respond in any particular situation.
4. It offers a precise, step-by-step technique for analysing all

types of handwriting – from long texts to a signature at the bottom of a typewritten letter. You will learn how to carry out the analysis without any need for jargon or subjective generalisations, and make predictions which are right to the point.

5. Graphonomy is founded in well-established scientific procedures, objective evidence derived from statistical analysis and the researches of large numbers of scientific investigators in the laboratories and universities of America and Europe. There is no need for intuition and no room for guesswork. Graphonomy is as precise as an electronic calculator.

6. Graphonomy is so easy to learn that mastering its procedures is, quite literally, child's play. In a pilot study by the authors, a group of ten-year-olds were given twenty minutes' instruction and then asked to analyse samples of handwriting. All made many correct predictions and more than 60% achieved almost complete accuracy.

HOW CAN HANDWRITING SAY SO MUCH?

Handwriting often says more about a person than a thousand well-chosen words. Every time we put pen to paper, whether to write a letter, scribble a note or make out a memo we betray ourselves in scores of subtle ways.

It is not *what* we write that matters but *how* the letters and words are formed. Every line of script contains clues about our inner selves which are as personal and unique as a set of fingerprints. The hidden language of handwriting is frequently more informative than a detailed biography and almost always far more revealing. For it can say things about a writer of which even they are blissfully unaware!

How can handwriting reveal so much? Why should the way we write prove to be such an accurate reflection of our true selves?

To answer these questions we need to look more closely at the exact nature of writing. Before doing so, carry out this simple task. Scribble your name on a scrap of paper.

How long did it take? Probably less than a couple of seconds. How much thought did you have to give to the task? Almost certainly very little. Signing your name is a simple, rapid, virtually automatic activity which you will have carried out hundreds, perhaps thousands, of times before. We asked you to write your name, rather than something requiring more thought, simply because it is one of the most mechanical pieces of writing we ever need to produce.

Although we may have to think very hard about the most appropriate words to use, translating them from thoughts to lines on a piece of paper usually requires little real mental effort. Whether we are writing a business proposal or a shopping list, a love letter or an examination answer, the words tend to unfold across the paper in obedience to the ideas running through our heads. Writing has become a well-worn habit.

The ease and speed of the mechanical aspects of writing conceal two important facts about the skill. The first is that this seemingly simple activity is extremely complex. Even the apparently straightforward business of signing your name makes considerable demands on brain and muscles. The second fact is that, because the body takes control over the writing process, it can say things our brains may not have been consciously aware of.

Let us examine these two components of handwriting by considering how the child learns to write. Early attempts are slow and painful. Each letter is printed out. The lines are wildly uneven, the words poorly formed. Then comes a stage in which words are joined up, line straightness improves and the letters take on a more specific and legible style. But it is still a process requiring considerable thought. Just as when we try to understand an imperfectly known language we must translate every word in our heads, so must the child concentrate both on the ideas behind the words and on creating the words themselves. Endless practice goes into shaping the letters and forming the words. As the ability becomes increasingly effortless and automatic the child begins to develop a style which differs from that taught in school. With increasing maturity, personality and other factors exert far more influence on the character of the handwriting than the early classroom-taught letter shapes. What emerges is an absolutely unique arrangement of line and loop, form and flow that distinguishes each individual's handwriting and makes it an absolutely unique production.

Producing any piece of writing, even something as short and straightforward as a signature, requires a highly co-ordinated series of movements by more than twenty muscles. Some are large and powerful, others no thicker than a cat's whisker and capable of making the most subtle and sensitive adjustments.

All the muscles must function in perfect synchrony in order to write effectively, and the brain has to integrate their different activities with the precision of an orchestra conductor. Just as in an orchestra one discordant note will be obvious to the trained ear, so in handwriting will one disharmony in the rhythm of script formation be glaringly apparent to the trained eye of the graphonomist. It may reveal itself in a particular letter formation; the presence or absence of certain strokes – as in the two examples we have already given – or the pressure used to form the words. It may appear as a hesitancy in letter strokes or in the size of the letters used. This impairment of harmony, whether it is due to temporary stress or long-term anxiety, current illness or impending disease, cannot be hidden by the writer. Indeed any attempts to do so will be just as revealing.

These variations in handwriting performance are preserved in the structure of the script, as what Dr. Philip Vernon has termed 'crystallised gesture'.

But how is it that internal disharmonies of which the writer is frequently unaware, can reveal themselves through the writing style?

As we have explained, some of the muscles used are very small and capable of tiny but precise movements. Like all the other muscles in the body they are controlled by the brain and nervous system. When the brain instructs the body to write, the muscles involved are set in motion by a stream of neural impulses. These are brief bursts of electricity which travel along the nerves. The flow of impulses, to even the smallest muscles, is a reflection of the state of the entire nervous system.

Because of this, any disturbance, however minor, in any part of the body influences the movements of the writing muscles and so effects the handwriting itself.

Often these disturbances are so slight they are like a whisper in a hurricane. Normally the multitude of other messages flowing through the system would overwhelm them, and no diagnostic equipment has yet been designed which is selective and sensitive enough to isolate and amplify them. The only way to gain early warning of such difficulties, which may be either physiological or psychological in nature, is to study the handwriting and learn to interpret its hidden language.

GRAPHONOMY IN ACTION

Let us now consider two aspects of handwriting in order to demonstrate how much the new procedures enable us to discover from what may, at first sight, appear to be trivial aspects of script formation. The starting point for our investigation is an indication, that is a characteristic of the handwriting, which you have probably seen scores of times before without ever appreciating its significance.

The Missing 'i' Dot

'Dot your 'i's and cross your 't's' must be the most basic rule any child is taught when learning to write. In primary school most children obey the teacher. But, later in life, some people drop the 'i' dots completely. Perhaps you have noticed this omission in your own, or somebody else's, handwriting. If so, you probably dismissed it as a sign of carelessness or haste. An occasional 'i' dot absence might well be due to forgetfulness or having to write in a hurry, but where this omission is a persistent feature of the script it has a great deal to tell us about the writer's personality.

In a study at Illinois State University, the missing 'i' dot was just one of fifty handwriting variables intensively examined by Dr. Elmer Lemke and Dr. John Kirchner. With the assistance of a computer they were able to analyse large numbers of samples and relate them to the personality of the writers concerned.

Their conclusion was the writers who habitually miss out the 'i' dot are not merely being absent-minded. They are deliberately trying to eliminate one part of the letter formation rules taught in primary school. In doing so they make a basic statement about their attitudes towards life. It is a tiny but significant rejection of authority, a rebellion against the need to conform. When they examined personality test results from such writers, Dr. Lemke and Dr. Kirchner found that they were less conventional and more imaginative in their attitude towards life. They tended to be self-confident and self-sufficient individualists. Despite this, they were not reserved when it came to social encounters. If anything they were adventurous, quite prepared to strike up conversations with strangers. But their need for people was not great and they could manage perfectly well on their own. In a later chapter we will describe what it would be like to have such an individual as an employer or employee, a friend, a marriage partner or a lover.

The psychologists also discovered a direct relationship between the frequency of missing 'i' dots and the extent to which these personality traits were exhibited by the writers. The greater the number of undotted 'i' strokes the less conventional or conformist the individual, the more independent and the greater the likelihood of their having a rich fantasy life.

This example of graphonomy in action illustrates how much can be learned from a seemingly trivial feature of the handwriting. Now let us consider a second, apparently equally insignificant, aspect of writing style which turns out to be no less revealing.

Anchor Strokes

Look at the words 'you'; and 'assess' in the sample below.

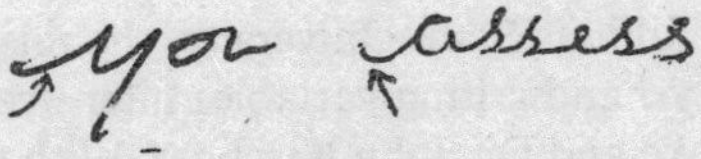

Fig. 1.

The arrows indicate how the writers have extended the first

stroke of each letter in the form of a small 'tail'. Why should they have chosen to do this? It is certainly not a standard writing movement taught in school, so clearly the embellishment has been added by the writer for some individual reason. A simple flourish to make the script more distinctive? An indication of an imaginative, unconventional individual?

The additional lines on the initial letters are called 'anchor strokes'. They curve down to the baseline of the writing and serve as 'props' by which the writer contrives to 'anchor' his writing to the line. It is important to distinguish between the curving lines, as illustrated, and other types of extension such as the straight line strokes illustrated below. These are no less important, and have just as much to tell us about the writer, but they are not 'anchor strokes'.

Fig. 2.

Why does the writer use such strokes? Research has shown that they provide a 'crutch' or 'support' for the word which is used to keep the words attached to the baseline, so helping to produce a fairly level line of writing.

So these somewhat unusual additions to initial letters serve a practical purpose for the writer. They make the finished work appear straighter and neater. But what do they tell us about those who use them?

A revealing study into the meaning of anchor strokes has been carried out by Dr. Lawrence Epstein at New York City's Columbia University. He found that writers using them showed distinct emotional and social attitudes. They tended to be more passive, less confident and less emotionally mature than writers who made no attempt at using anchor strokes. They were more conformist, both in their judgements and the way they responded to situations. They had a greater acceptance of conventional expressions of authority and placed a high value on power in others. They expressed the opinion that individuals should be expected to fall in with the wishes of family members or anybody in authority. They were eager to conform to social pressures and opinions. When confronted by a problem which they found tough to handle, the users of anchor strokes were very likely to withdraw rather than actively attempt to deal with the situation.

They were not very self-contained individuals and needed to express their feelings to others, although they handled irrational feelings, particularly powerful emotions, by denying them. There was a tendency for them to feel deprived in the emotional relationships with their fathers.

Dr. Epstein also discovered that writers who used anchor strokes tended to hold dogmatic opinions and had difficulty in accepting logical conclusions if these conflicted with their own views. These firm opinions were associated with a straight-forward approach to life which led them to express their views openly and unhesitatingly. They were ambitious and would use their assertive natures to satisfy these ambitions, but only so long as this could be accomplished according to prescribed conventions. They generally did not seek to get ahead by challenging what they regard as any legitimate authority.

So on the basis of this single sign we can build up a fairly detailed portrait of the writer. He, or she, will be likely to have strong views which they express frankly. But their opinions will be conformist and never seek to challenge authority. They will be easily swayed by the views of others, especially their superiors. Their conventional outlook will be matched by a conformist appearance and they will tend to be dogmatic and excessively critical, especially of their employees. But they go out of their way to please their own bosses and never take the risk of arousing the displeasure of those above them. In their private lives they will be eager to form relationships but may find it hard to let themselves go emotionally. They will prefer to keep back something of themselves from even the most intimate companion.

This may seem a remarkably large amount of information to

gather from such a seemingly minor aspect of handwriting. But Dr. Epstein's meticulous research has clearly established this pattern of personality in *anchor stroke* stroke users. As you learn more about graphonomy, you will discover that a wealth of detail can be gleaned from tell-tale handwriting signs so small that you might previously never even have noticed them.

CARRYING OUT A FULL ANALYSIS

We have already seen how two seemingly trivial aspects of the way in which a person writes, missing 'i' dots and *anchor strokes*, can tell us a great deal about personality. We have also suggested a few of the ways in which threats to our health and happiness may be detected in handwriting. Now we will bring together a number of graphonomy procedures to illustrate how it is possible to build up a meaningful picture of an individual's lifestyle from a brief sample of writing. To do so, we will draw on our example from our research files.

Michael – Executive Under Pressure

The short sample of handwriting below belongs to an executive we shall call Michael. At the time he wrote those words he was fifty-five years old and held an important position in a New York publishing house.

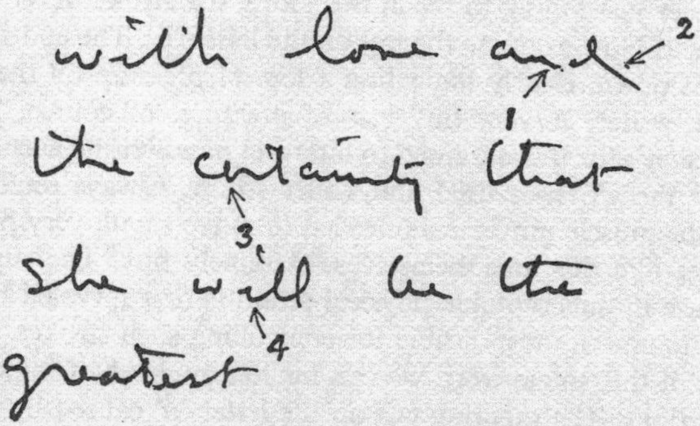

Fig. 3.

We would like you to examine those dozen words carefully and try to decide if they tell you anything significant. Remember it is not *what* is written that counts but *how* the words have been constructed.

Probably there is not much you can find in the writing. Indeed, we suspect that if you received a letter written like that tomorrow you would hardly give it a second glance. In fact those dozen words formed the basis of advice which was offered to Michael. Advice which he was wise enough to take. Advice which, it seems fairly certain, saved his life.

The Analysis

When Michael came for an analysis of his handwriting he seemed in perfect health. Although he drove himself hard and was under a great deal of pressure, Michael appeared to thrive on such a life-style. But while there were no outward signs of physical distress, such indications were clearly evident in his handwriting.

Look carefully at the word 'and', on the example of his handwriting. Arrows one and two point out the significant aspects. Notice, first of all, how the downward stroke on the letter 'n' falls away and fails to join up with the letter 'd'. The tip of this stroke is rising slightly as if there had been an attempt to make contact with the next letter. However, like an exhausted swimmer just failing to reach the shore, the stroke never quite makes it. Now examine the tail on the letter 'd'. The end stroke droops down, clearly indicating a loss of pressure on the part of the writer. A very tiny loss of pressure, of course, but a clear sign – for those trained to interpret handwriting accurately – that the writer is tired and under strain. Always remember that the muscle movements needed to make small, very precise strokes like this are, themselves, extremely tiny. The slightest increase in unacceptable physical strain is first revealed by the delicate muscles responsible for controlling such strokes.

From this single word we can make a number of important deductions. The tapering tail on the letter 'n' caused by a loss of pressure on the part of the writer. As a result the writing impulse, which should carry the line through to the letter 'd' loses momentum. In the effort needed to complete the 'd', the writer shows a similar 'exhaustion'. The forward impetus has disappeared causing an exaggerated droop and pressure loss.

Extensive research evidence shows that end-stroke droop and a loss of pressure are two of the most significant indications of excessive stress and fatigue.

These were not symptoms of which Michael was aware. So far as he was concerned his body was standing up perfectly to the daily pressures of executive living. He did not feel himself overtired or under a dangerous amount of strain. But those normally unnoticed traces of stress in his handwriting were like the trace peaks on the seismographic recorder. What they were quite clearly saying was that, somewhere in his system, tremors were occurring.

Now let us look at the ways in which Michael shaped the 'i' in the word 'will' and the 'e' in 'certainty' (arrows three and four). Here we find confirmation of the warnings present in the earlier words. The connecting strokes between the 'e' and 'r' in 'certainty', and the 'i' and the 'l' in 'will' reveal an unmistakable tendency to droop.

Research has shown that such drooping is an early indication of depression. Certainly Michael's briskly confident manner gave no suggestion that he was depressed. Yet the message of his handwriting was clear, and was made even more significant by the rhythm and fluency which characterises the rest of his writing. When studying small details of handwriting it is important to keep in mind any similarities or differences with the whole.

So the sample tells us that Michael is under long-term stress and not standing up to it as well as he believes. He also has a tendency towards depression and might do well to widen his range of interests to provide more varied stimulation.

But that is not all those twelve words have to say about their writer. Within that short sample are slightly more ominous indications of health problems. The way in which the word 'greatest' has been written provides the vital clue. In order to clarify the main points we have magnified the word eight times.

The letter 'g' begins with a faint, weak stroke before thickening out to form the loop. Weakness of pressure at the start or end of a letter stroke are clear indicators of stress.

This need not be all that serious. In the absence of other signs, such a loss of pressure might only show that the writer was going through a period of excessive, short-term stress. But combined with the other indications already described, this strongly suggests that Michael is suffering from the effects of prolonged and unacceptably high levels of stress. There is also a clear indication that this may be having serious consequences for his long-term health.

Examine the pen stroke which connects the letters 'e' and 'a'. (Indicated by arrow.) You will see that the line appears uneven. There is a 'ropiness' in the stroke, with wavy edges giving the appearance of a length of hawser. This tendency to ropiness, the technical term is segmentation, is also just visible in the final stroke of the letter 't' (arrowed).

Segmentation is caused by a minute tremor in the smallest muscle groups utilised in writing. This tremor is, in turn, an indication of deeper disturbances within the nervous system. They warn of more than temporary stress effects and suggest the early stage of a serious physical difficulty. How and why this occurs will be described fully in chapter eight when we look at ways in which handwriting acts as a mirror for one's overall health.

In order to interpret segmentation accurately, it is essential to note how frequently it occurs in the sample and to look for other indicators of ill-health. When there is a large amount of segmentation, the writer is likely to have serious and immediate health problems. However, in Michael's case the extent of the segmentation is minor, which showed that his difficulties were still at a very early stage.

Once segmentation had been detected, a careful examination was made of the letter angles, these are the sharp turns which the writer must execute in order to form certain letters, for example the loop of the 'g' and the stroke of the 't'.

Fig. 4.

If he had been unable to make sharp turns, the evidence would have suggested a certain type of physical problems which we will discuss in chapter eight. However, the major indications in his handwriting, a poor pressure cycle, segmentation and the ability to make sharp letter turns, are often associated with heart trouble.

The hidden language of Michael's handwriting told us this. Here was a busy, ambitious executive whose mental and physical condition was not quite as good as he believed it to be. Although he seemed happy and self-assured there were warnings of depression. There were also signs that the pressured lifestyle was having a greater effect on his health than he appreciated, with indications of long-term pressure effects and a suggestion of heart disease. On the basis of this analysis Michael was advised to ease up slightly, to widen his range of interests and to have medicals every six months incorporating special checks for heart trouble. Michael took the advice. For two years he was given a clean bill of health by the doctors. Then, to his dismay if not his complete surprise, a check-up revealed heart disease at a very early stage. Thanks to the early detection, prompt and effective remedial action was taken. Today, five years later, Michael is still in an excellent state of health.

HOW GRAPHONOMY CAN HELP YOU

We have already described some of the ways in which graph-onomy is being used to provide important information about a person's physical and mental health, personality traits, levels of intellectual ability, and social attitudes. No doubt many practical applications for graphonomy in your own life have already occurred to you. But here are ten areas in which our clients and students have found the thorough and scientifically validated procedures of this new technique especially valuable.

* Within the family for keeping a regular check on mental and physical health. All it requires is a sample of handwriting, a little time and the knowledge which the book will provide.

* To monitor changes in stress levels in yourself, your family or your work associates. Graphonomy enables you to discover

whether these pressures are producing a long-lasting or only a short-term difficulty.

* To keep a check on children, especially at critical periods of their lives. When starting a new school, for example; after a period of sickness; before important examinations and at any other time when they may be under abnormal stress.

* To determine whether a writer is sincere in what he, or she, is saying. Does the way the words are formed tell a different story to what the words themselves are saying?

* To assess the personality of the writer. This can prove invaluable to employers hiring staff for senior positions or jobs requiring a particular type of individual, for example somebody who relates well to other people or a person who can do routine tasks painstakingly.

* To discover what sort of attitudes towards life the writer is likely to hold and so find out what kind of a boss, friend, spouse or lover they would make. Graphonomy can go a long way towards telling you.

* To check on the emotional stability of somebody who figures prominently in either your business or your private life. Are they likely to prove well-balanced or unreliable; conventional or nonconformist? What about your own emotional make-up? How well do you really know yourself? A simple analysis of your handwriting may reveal things about your own innermost feelings which you have never known before.

* To indicate levels of intellectual ability in adults or children. Handwriting samples can provide a very accurate guide not merely to an individual's level of intelligence but also the amount of imagination and creativity they are likely to show when solving problems. You can use these graphonomy procedures to estimate your own, or anybody else's, mental capacity.

* To analyse signatures and find out how the writer really views the world. In these days of typewritten letters the most we normally see of a writer's individual style comes in the often scrawled signature. But, brief though the sample usually is,

it can tell us a great deal about the person who wrote it. In business it may provide a vital clue as to how best to deal with an associate, a customer or a competitor.

* Finally, and for many users of graphonomy most crucially, the new science provides an early and reliable early warning of long-term health problems. Thanks to the analysis of his handwriting, Michael was able to take effective action to reduce his day-to-day stress and act promptly to contain the risks involved in his executive lifestyle. It makes sense for anybody under regular pressure to carry out the same, simple checks.

We must, however, point out that while these indications of ill-health are extremely accurate when correctly identified and interpreted, it would be quite wrong to regard them as a conclusive diagnosis. They provide an indication of health problems which must be confirmed by a conventional medical examination. Only a qualified doctor is in a position to make such a diagnosis or offer such confirmation.

THE USES AND ABUSES OF GRAPHONOMY

Before we describe how you should set about learning to use this exciting new science we think it only right to offer these words of caution. Graphonomy is a system for analysing handwriting which has been developed from a wide range of research studies. It is the first time that these powerful procedures have been made generally available and, as with any valid method of psychological assessment, knowledge of such techniques places considerable power in the hands of those who have mastered them.

While we see nothing objectionable in using such a system as a means of entertaining as well as informing, it would be quite wrong to look on graphonomy as some kind of parlour game. The matters with which it deals, and the knowledge provided, will often be of great importance to those concerned. For example, when you are able to accurately assess an individual's emotional condition, their responses to stress or their risk of serious illness; when you find it possible to discover the true quality of their personal relationships or intellectual abilities.

We hope that once you have learned how to use graphonomy correctly you will be prepared to abide by these six golden rules of interpretation:

(1) Under no circumstances should the knowledge which has been gained be used to embarrass or distress anybody.

(2) All information obtained should be regarded as confidential and used only for ethical purposes.

(3) When disclosing the results of your analysis to the writer concerned – which you will almost certainly be called on to do in most instances – use considerable tact and discretion if conveying anything negative about their personality or abilities. If in doubt – leave it out!

(4) If you come to any conclusions about the writer's state of health – and as we have shown, graphonomy does allow the diagnosis of many major medical problems – be even more cautious. Never say anything which could cause alarm or unnecessary concern. Revealing such findings requires a tremendous amount of care and tact. Remember that only a person qualified by long years of medical training and experience of diseases is in a position to fully understand health problems.

(5) Practice the methods we describe until you are confident of your ability to carry out a successful analysis and only *then* offer to give any public demonstrations of your new skills. If you are unable to analyse a particular word or piece of script to your satisfaction, then admit as much. Never give in to the temptation to invent some glib answer in order to gloss over a lack of knowledge.

(6) If possible try to find out the conditions under which a sample of writing was made. Were they such as to distort the script in some way which might mislead you, for instance if written on a rough surface, while travelling by train and so on? You should also try to determine the writer's sex because this could well influence the final interpretation and, probably, the way you will want to present the information. Never form a

final judgement on some important topic – for example the writer's emotional state, health, or the nature of a relationship – on the basis of a single sample. Analyse several pieces of writing by the same individual and try to ensure that your conclusions are not coloured by any personal attitudes or anxieties.

By following these simple rules you will find that the analysis of handwriting can only prove a valuable and rewarding experience.

So let us make a start. In chapter two we will describe the few items of simple equipment needed to carry out an analysis and outline the basic procedures which will enable you to begin your own interpretations of the hidden language of handwriting.

Chapter Two

Making a Start

The procedures of graphonomy were developed by researchers using a wide range of sophisticated equipment. In order to identify and validate many of the more subtle characteristics of the hidden language it was necessary to use computers, ultrasensitive balances, microscopes, high-power magnifiers and precision-measuring instruments. Such elaborate technology was essential in order to produce data which satisfied the exacting demands of scientific enquiry.

Fortunately you do not need anything complex or costly in order to carry out a successful analysis of all types of handwriting! Now that the techniques have been perfected they can be used with only a minimum of delay and difficulty. Such equipment as is necessary can easily be obtained, and you may already own most of what is required.

EQUIPPING YOURSELF FOR GRAPHONOMY

In order to be able to interpret handwriting accurately you need a total of just eight simple items. This includes the two most basic and essential pieces of equipment – something to write with and something to write on.

You can analyse handwriting no matter how it has been produced. It is not important whether the writer worked with a fountain pen or a biro, a fibre tip or a pencil, a crayon or a stick of chalk. One can even analyse handwriting which has been sprayed onto a wall using an aerosol paint can!

This is possible because of a remarkable feature of our handwriting. No matter how the words are written down an individual's style, once formed, remains constant. Even if a writer started a sentence using a fine-nibbed pen and completed it with a piece of charcoal, the underlying characteristics – what are termed the indicators or indices of a handwriting sample – would be preserved.

This is the main reason why handwriting examination is such a valuable part of criminal detection. Forged documents, blackmail notes, threatening letters, even a faked signature, can usually be linked to a particular writer through these unalterable indicators. No matter how hard a person tries to disguise his writing, the unique indices survive. It has even been possible to identify vandals responsible for daubing walls with graffiti by comparing the brush-smeared words with the writer's normal script.

The remarkable persistence of style was demonstrated by a recent study which looked at the writings of men and women who, through accident or disease, had become paralysed. Because they were no longer able to hold the pen conventionally they had developed a variety of writing techniques. Some gripped it between their teeth and wrote with head movements, others used their toes and feet. When comparisons were made of their writing styles before and after the paralysis, it was found that the underlying characteristics remained constant.

This happens because handwriting is a well-practised skill, a habit acquired so perfectly that it has become what psychologists term – *overlearned*. Fixed patterns of commands are established within the brain which determine the sequence of actions needed to form any letter or word. Even when the muscle groups used are changed, as in the case of the paralysed writers, the same basic sequence of commands is transmitted from the brain. This continues to happen even when the writer deliberately tries to alter his, or her, style.

When you have learned how to use graphonomy to analyse handwriting, therefore, you have no reason to worry about how a script sample was produced or concern yourself that the writer was trying to mislead you by changing writing styles. You will still be able to carry out an accurate analysis and your predictions will be just as valid.

THE WRITING INSTRUMENT

Fountain Pens - Steel Nib Pens

While all we have said about the persistence of handwriting characteristics holds true no matter what writing instrument is used, it must be added that script produced using ink and either a fountain pen or an old fashioned steel nibbed pen, will yield the most information. This is because the flexible steel or platinum points are extremely sensitive to the amount of force applied in forming the letter strokes. The most minute and subtle variations in pressure are transmitted to the paper in the form of changes in ink density or stroke width. As a result the handwriting accurately reflects the ebb and flow of the writing pressure in a way which cannot be achieved using a more rigid writing point, for instance a biro or fibre-tip. These pressure variations are important as they provide a reliable indication of the writer's internal mental and physical condition. They are especially valuable in identifying short- or long-term stress problems and in predicting the probable response to a crisis.

Biros

Much of the handwriting you want to analyse is likely to have been produced by the widely-used biro. Such samples can provide a great deal of information, although it is necessary to take care when assessing pressure changes. Methods by which this can be achieved will be fully described in the next chapter.

Fibre-Tip Pens

Because of the smooth action of this kind of pen, much stiffness or jerkiness in the handwriting is concealed. This is the main reason why people with poor handwriting often prefer to use such pens. The finished appearance of the script tends to be more attractive and satisfying than they could obtain with a biro or fountain pen. It does present some problems of analysis, however. Pressure changes become even harder to detect than in biro script.

As we will explain in chapter three, pressure is an important and revealing characteristic. Other indicators of style remain as easily detectable as in other types of script.

Pencil

This form of writing is difficult to interpret as regards pressure variations but satisfactory in all other respects.

Crayon

Most of the crayon-writing you come across will probably have been produced by children who have only just learned how to write. It is not possible to detect pressure changes in crayon but the flow of the writing and other important indications are well preserved. Analysing this kind of handwriting can be valuable and rewarding, providing important insights into the minds of the young, as we will explain in chapter nine.

THE WRITING PAPER

The best material for collecting samples are sheets of white, unlined paper of medium thickness. The kind used in memo pads or for typing letters is ideal. White paper is preferable because it shows up variations in script density most readily, and being unlined, one can assess the writer's ability to produce accurately aligned letters and words. The significance of line straightness will be discussed in chapters seven and nine. If you decide to monitor your handwriting on a daily basis, as we will suggest, then a notebook of white, unlined paper provides the most practical form of record keeping. This type of regular check is an excellent way of keeping an eye on changing stress levels and as a means of anticipating possible health hazards.

With these most basic items out of the way let us consider the six remaining items of inexpensive equipment needed in order to carry out a full analysis of all types of handwriting.

Magnifying Glass

Most of what we term the *macromovements* of handwriting,

that is the major indicators, can be detected and examined with the naked eye. However there are some *micromovements*, the products of very subtle neural activity, which can only be studied using a magnifying glass. You will find this especially important when using the analysis to look for signs of unacceptable stress levels or impending ill-health.

For much of the work a fairly lower power glass (ie around ×3 magnification) will be adequate. There will, however, be occasions when a more powerful lens is needed (a ×7 or ×10 glass is usually satisfactory). The ×8 magnification of the word 'greatest' in the previous chapter shows how much can be discovered from an enlargement.

Ruler

This is needed not to make measurements – none are necessary when carrying out an analysis – but in order to check the straightness of lines of handwriting. A transparent, plastic ruler is easier to use than a wood or metal one because it allows several lines to be scanned at the same time.

Watch

One of the tests which we will be describing in later chapters have to be timed in seconds. A wristwatch with a sweep second hand, a digital watch which indicates seconds or a stop watch will be needed.

Carbon Paper

Two sheets of ordinary black or blue-black carbon paper. The size is not important, provided it is large enough to make copies of a reasonable length of script. You can buy carbon paper at a stationers' or office supply store.

Carbon paper is useful because the images which it produces have more contrast than can be obtained by the direct action of a pen or biro. This means that changes in pressure and shades of pressure are reproduced on the carbon copy as clearly distinguished light and dark tones, so making them easier to interpret.

Lightweight Paper Pad

This pad should contain very lightweight writing paper, the kind used to send airmail letters is ideal. If you are unable to find such a pad, you can buy individual sheets of airmail paper and put these together in a way which we will describe in the next chapter, to carry out a handwriting pressure test.

Graph Tracing Paper

This is the only thing needed for graphonomy which could be considered specialised. Graph tracing paper consists of sheets of translucent material with a standard graph paper grid over-printed. It means that when you place the sheet down on a sample of handwriting it is easy to make out the words beneath the superimposed grid. You will be able to purchase graph tracing paper from almost any art or technical drawing supply store. Ask for sheets of A4 size with 12 squares to the inch.

Graph tracing paper has two main uses in graphonomy. It can be used for measuring and comparing signature sizes. We shall be describing how and why this is done in chapter five where we will also provide standard reference signatures for quick comparison. Graph tracing paper is also useful when estimating variations in handwriting size, an important fact or which will be explained later in the book. Although graph tracing paper may look complicated when you first see it, using it for handwriting analysis is simplicity itself.

This is the only equipment needed. Once you have these items you will be ready to carry out all types of analysis. Before starting off, however, it is important to consider some of the ground rules which should be followed if graphonomy is to be used correctly.

AVOID ...
OVERGENERALISATIONS

No form of psychological assessment can claim 100% accuracy, and this applies to IQ and personality tests just as much to graphonomy. One can say with confidence however that the objectively validated procedures of this method of assessment are as reliable as any in use today. In some areas, for example personality, handwriting analysis has received far more convincing experimental support than have many of the more popular tests widely used by psychologists.

SEEK . . .
CONFIRMATIONS

Do not consider single aspects of the handwriting in isolation. look for confirmation elsewhere in the sample before reaching any conclusions. Seek out further, similar characteristics, or indications which carry the same meaning. For example, you may remember we described the way in which missing 'i' dots are typically found in the handwriting of people who are nonconformists and independent. But you should not attach too much significance to a single missing 'i' dot. It might simply mean that the writer was distracted for a moment. However, if the single missing 'i' dot was just one of a number of indications of independence and nonconformity it would be quite correct to take it into account.

Try to approach all handwriting with an open mind. You will usually know something, perhaps a great deal, about the person who produced the sample. But search for your information within the writing and remain as objective as possible. Here again an emphasis on confirmation for each conclusion you reach will help to prevent major errors of interpretation.

CONSIDER . . .
THE BIG PICTURE

When arriving at a final assessment look at *all* the indications present in the handwriting.

Do not focus your attention on only one or two of them and ignore the remainder.

Do not choose to ignore certain characteristics because they fail to fit in with your conclusions.

Do not be content until you have explored every aspect of the sample. Gain experience using your own handwriting and, perhaps, that of close friends, before embarking on a serious analysis of handwriting, from which you are going to draw important conclusions. Building up skill and knowledge in graphonomy is largely a matter of experience. There can be no short cuts. You will find it helpful to carry out the interpretation exercise at the end of chapter ten. This practice session will help you gain confidence and knowledge without running the risk of making an embarrassing, and perhaps hurtful, mistake. The most effective way to see the big picture is to use what we term the funnel technique. This means starting out by focusing on the more global aspects of the sample and then narrowing your attention down to consider smaller and smaller details in the script (see facing page).

With these simple items of equipment at hand you are now ready to begin learning how to analyse handwriting using the powerful procedures of graphonomy, and there is no better place to start than with your own handwriting. So before you read the next chapter, here is what we would like you to do.

Take a sheet of white, unlined paper and place it either on a pad or a magazine so that you do not have to write directly on a hard surface. Now, with medium-nibbed fountain pen, write about half a page of spontaneous script. It does not matter *what* you write. Remember it is only how you form the letters and words that is important. If you are stuck for a subject you could do worse than fall back on an old device used by broadcasters when they want to obtain a voice level before making a recording. Then the speaker is simply asked to recall what he, or she, had for breakfast. When you have completed half a page of handwriting, write your name, using your usual signature.

Now you should turn to the next chapter where we will explain how you can carry out some of the most fundamental procedures in graphonomy – pressure checks. Their purpose is to enable you to determine activity and stress levels, two key aspects of everybody's personality and lifestyle.

THE FUNNEL SYSTEM OF ANALYSIS

Overall Appearance

Aspects of the handwriting to be considered initially include such factors of general appearance as the flow. This includes the fluency of the writing and the continuity of the forward movement. You must also examine the overall pressure used to produce the sample; the originality of style which the writer has developed and the speed with which the sample was produced. Other characteristics add measurably to the overall impression of a sample: You should pay particular attention to legibility, how the writer corrected any errors, and the size of the signature. These will be discussed in later chapters.

Internal Structure

With the general appearance noted, and all the available information obtained, you can now study aspects of the internal structure of the script. These include variations of pressure within words, variations in slant, and variations of letter size and shape. It is the characteristics of internal structure which begin to distinguish one writer from another.

Fine Detail

Finally, you have to consider the subtle and highly personal features of script. These may be likened to fingerprints in their individuality. They include distinctive details such as momentary interruptions of the writing flow, isolated pressure variations, and unique anomalies of co-ordination.

Chapter Three

What You Predict From Handwriting Pressure

The amount of pressure used in writing varies considerably from person to person and research has shown that it accurately reflects the way in which the writer will respond to many of the demands and difficulties of everyday life. It is one of the most important aspects of handwriting and the first thing you should consider when carrying out an analysis.

In order to interpret handwriting pressure successfully, it is essential to consider these three key factors:

1. The overall level of pressure typically used by the writer.
2. The way in which that pressure is distributed throughout the script.
3. Variations in overall pressure which occur as a result of the writer's mental and physical response to stress.

In this chapter we will be looking at each of these factors in turn; describing how to carry out simple tests which provide a rapid but reliable guide to pressure levels and variations, and explaining how to relate these indications to everyday life. You will discover exactly what to expect if certain pressure characteristics are present in the handwriting of your employer, or an employee, a marriage partner, a friend or an intimate companion.

The first aspect to consider when starting an analysis is overall pressure.

OVERALL PRESSURE

By this we mean the *average* amount of pressure which the writer is accustomed to use. A person who expends a great deal of energy and effort in their everyday activities will put an equal amount of intensity into his handwriting. In the case of someone who is very active and vigorous this intensity will be released through the degree of downward force used on the pen. This greater pressure provides a reliable indication of the writer's general activity level.

The best place to begin your analysis is by carrying out one or more of the simple pressure check tests below.

HOW TO CHECK HANDWRITING PRESSURE

The Touch Test

This is the simplest and quickest of all tests to carry out, but it will only work with samples written in biro or pencil. Simply slide your fingers under the paper and notice whether or not you can feel the impression made by the writing. It is of course important to take the thickness of the paper into account when carrying out the touch test. But you will find this comes quite easily with a little practice. Highly active individuals will produce handwriting which leaves easily-felt indentations.

The Intensity Index

This is a slightly longer but rather more accurate pressure test which you can apply to handwriting samples produced by fountain pen or biro. Study *The Intensity Index* below and note which of the lines comes closest in darkness and width to the greater part of the handwriting which you want to analyse. You should not make the comparison with either the lightest or the darkest strokes in the script but try to select those which seem most representative of the writing as a whole.

The five lines in each index are graded in order of pressure, the lightest on the top and the heaviest on the bottom. These comparison keys, which have been developed from our own research, provide a standard against which you can determine the pressure level of any handwriting sample. With the fountain pen index you will notice that, reading from left to right, lines show a marked increase in width, as well as darkness, and this should be taken into account when making the comparison.

Intensity Index

Index One Use these samples for comparison if the hand-writing is in fountain pen.	Index Two Use these samples if the handwriting is in biro.
Line One ———————— Fig. 1.	*Line One* ———————— Fig. 2.
Line Two ———————— Fig. 3.	*Line Two* ———————— Fig. 4.
Line Three ———————— Fig. 5.	*Line Three* ———————— Fig. 6.
Line Four ———————— Fig. 7.	*Line Four* ———————— Fig. 8.
Line Five ———————— Fig. 9.	*Line Five* ———————— Fig. 10.

Once you have made the comparison, using the appropriate index for the type of handwriting being analysed, refer the line selected to the chart below to discover the meaning of that level of overall pressure.

Intensity Chart

Line One: Very light pressure. The writer has a low energy level. Will be generally sluggish and unwilling to engage in strenuous physical activity for extended periods. Prefers to go at own pace. Tends to let others take the initiative. Laconic and lacking in enthusiasm. But has a high tolerance of set-backs and frustrations and is unlikely to over-react at moments of crisis.

Line Two: Light pressure. The writer is below average in activity. Prefers to avoid situations which demand exertion for more than a short period. Both Line One and Line Two writers usually have a more realistic self-image than is found in writers showing higher levels of activity.

Line Three: Normal pressure. This represents the average handwriting pressure, and activity level, for the population. Most handwriting samples will correspond in density to this line. The writer is able to maintain a realistic balance between under- and over-exertion.

Line Four: Heavy pressure. Above average activity level. The writer enjoys having plenty to do and dislikes being delayed or obstructed. Has a need to be able to work off excess energy in an active occupation or leisure pursuit.

Line Five: Very heavy pressure. A highly active individual. Likes to be constantly on the move at work or at play. A go-getter who takes the initiative in most activities. Is in danger of expending efforts in too many directions at once. Has a low tolerance for frustrations and could easily become a victim of excessive stress.

This test offers an accurate indication of a writer's activity level. You can use it with confidence on the majority of samples since handwriting pressure generally remains more or less constant. There are, however, occasions when pressure will alter because of exceptional stress or serious illness. Although the majority of handwriting samples will match the interpretations we have given, you should always bear this possibility in mind when making an interpretation. Later in this chapter, and in chapter eight, we will explain how these variations occur and how you can interpret them.

The Pressure Pad Test

The above tests can be used to analyse any sample of handwriting. This test, although it gives very accurate results, is slightly more involved. Instead of being able to work directly from a finished script, you must make your assessment of a writer's pressure level by means of a pressure pad made up from twelve sheets of very lightweight airmail-type paper. You will also need a sheet of carbon paper the same size as the writing material being used.

How to Make a Pressure Pad

The completed pad is shown in the illustration (Figure 11) below. It consists of a sheet of normal weight, white, unlined paper on top of which has been placed a sheet of carbon paper and the twelve pieces of very lightweight paper.

Now write, or get your subject to write, in biro on the top sheet. It does not matter what is written, provided it is not their name and address. Only four or five words are necessary but the same ones must be used throughout the test.

When you have written on the first sheet, examine the normal weight paper at the bottom of the pile. Is it possible to detect any trace of the words on this sheet? You need not be able to read the words, merely to detect a ghost-like image *of about half the handwriting*.

If there are no such signs, remove the top sheet, write on the second piece of lightweight paper and check the bottom piece of paper again. Carry on doing this until a faint image of half the writing can be seen. Figure 12 shows how this test is carried out. As soon as a trace of the writing can be made out, stop

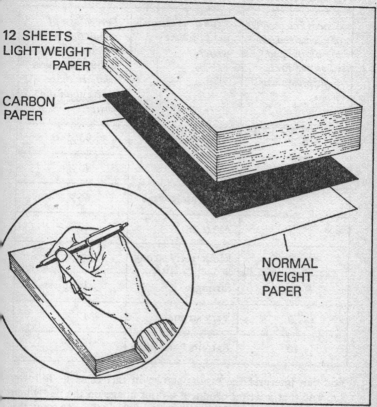

12 SHEETS LIGHTWEIGHT PAPER

CARBON PAPER

NORMAL WEIGHT PAPER

Fig. 11

the test and count how many sheets of lightweight paper remain in the pad. This gives you the *Pressure Score* for that writer. By referring the score to the chart below you will be able to discover the type of pressure used by the writer and how it compares to the rest of the population.

Pressure Chart

Score (The number of sheets remaining on the pad when the first, faint image was seen).	Type of pressure used by that writer.	Percentage of population with greater handwriting pressure, who are more active than the writer.
0–3	Very weak	95%
4	Weak	75%
5	Moderately weak	65%
6	Average	50%
7	Moderately strong	35%
8	Strong	15%
9	Very strong	12%
10	Extremely strong	5%

You can interpret the results shown in this chart as follows. Suppose that a writer produces a faint image on the pad when there are nine sheets left on the pad. This tells you that the writer uses *very strong* pressure and is in the top 12% of the population for writing pressure and activity level. He, or she, will be extremely energetic and vigorous in all areas of life. At the other end of the scale, if an image of the writing can only be seen after the pad has been reduced to three sheets, the writer uses *very weak* pressure and will be less active than 95% of the population.

The relationship between handwriting pressure and activity

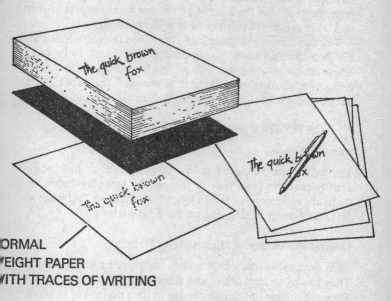

ORMAL
EIGHT PAPER
ITH TRACES OF WRITING

Fig. 12

levels was first investigated by Dr. Gerald Pascal, former head of Harvard University's Psychological Clinic, and has since been confirmed by a number of other studies including research carried out by one of the authors (James Greene) using several hundred subjects.

WHAT HANDWRITING PRESSURE PREDICTS

Pressure in the handwriting is a reflection of the writer's general activity level. This, in turn, has a profound influence over almost every aspect of the individual's lifestyle. It determines the type of job for which they are best suited and the sort of leisure activities most likely to be enjoyed. Once we have accurately assessed any writer's activity level it will be possible to predict the kind of behaviour we can expect of them in a wide range of everyday roles and situations.

The two basic tests described above, the Intensity Index and the Pressure Pad allow such a reliable assessment to be made. They enable us to place the writer in one of three activity categories, to discover what sort of attitudes they are likely to adopt towards life and find out how best to relate to them.

CATEGORY ONE – HIGH ACTIVITY LEVEL

Pressure Guide

The writer can be placed in this category if their handwriting density matches lines *four* or *five* on the Intensity Index or if there are *eight or more* sheets left on the Pressure Pad when the first, faint image is detected on the final sheet.

General Personality of High Activity Writers

Such writers will be hardworking, enthusiastic and go-getters. They like to be kept active and stimulated by anything they do. They are unable to tolerate routine or long periods of inactivity.

How You Will Relate to Them:

As your superior:
If your superior has a high level of activity you will be expected to be equally enthusiastic, hard-working and dedicated to the job as they are. Such people tend to work long hours and become irritated when others refuse to follow their example. They will approach all challenges with energy, determination and singlemindedness. They are always eager to tackle fresh projects and will take on as many as possible. When putting across their ideas such writers are more likely to use forceful persuasion rather than quiet diplomacy!

They will be intolerant of employees who appear to be under-occupied or idle, so if you like a quiet life at least try to give the appearance of being overwhelmed with work! To make yourself popular try to come up with a constant flow of fresh ideas and fling yourself wholeheartedly into any new scheme.

If you too have a high activity level you should get along well with this type of superior. If you have a medium activity level then life may be tolerable much of the time. But beware of working under such an individual if your activity level is low. You will soon become exhausted by their ceaseless demands and weary of their constant enthusiasms.

As your employee:

While a high level of activity is clearly desirable in many occupations it can actually prove a disadvantage in others. Such individuals will work best in jobs which give them plenty of stimulation and fresh challenges. Work which brings them into contact with members of the public, for example in selling, journalism or public relations should suit them well and they will remain interested and energetic. When highly motivated by a challenge which gives them the opportunity to burn up all that excess energy such people often excel. However, tasks which demand patient attention to detail and many routine chores, or jobs where there is plenty of brain work but very little leg-work, may soon make them restless for a change.

If you are a high activity person then avoid any career which does not offer a good level of physical exertion and a regular source of fresh stimulation.

As your marriage partner:

High activity people, whether men or women, tend not to be homebodies. They are seldom happy with any one furnishing scheme or décor for long and will constantly desire to change and experiment with their home environment. They will relish shifting things around, repainting and reorganising. Even after a hard day at work they will usually have sufficient reserves of energy to come home and, instead of settling down by the TV or with a book, will want to be finding something more physically demanding. If their interests lie outside the home then all this activity potential will be invested in that pursuit which may leave them little time for their spouse.

If you too have a high activity level then there should be no problems, and if you enjoy shared interests then the marriage should run smoothly. But watch out if your own activity level turns out to be on the low side. You could find yourself feeling either dreadfully exhausted or painfully neglected before long.

As your friend:
Providing you enjoy an active life then such a person will prove a stimulating companion. If you would prefer to stay quietly at home, then the conflict between your needs and theirs could quickly place the friendship under a severe strain. If you are a low activity person then the relationship may well be doomed. If you have a medium level of activity then you may find them excellent companions provided you do not have to spend all your free time in their company.

As your lover:
Provided that the high activity level lover has not used up too much energy at work or in some other pursuit your sex life should be vigorous if somewhat demanding. Their physical involvement and enthusiasm for sex may, however, be combined with a certain lack of romantic ability and an impatience with foreplay. They will want to dispense with the trappings and concentrate on the sexual act itself. They are likely to prove dominant both in bed and out of it and will probably insist on taking the lead in sexual activities. If you are a high or medium activity person then you should enjoy the relationship. But they could prove too demanding for somebody with a very low activity level.

CATEGORY TWO – MEDIUM ACTIVITY LEVEL

Pressure Guide

The writer can be placed in this category if their handwriting density matches *line three* on the Intensity Index or if there are *six or seven sheets* remaining on the Pressure Pad when the first, faint image is detected on the final sheet.

General Personality of Medium Activity Writers

Such writers will be able to maintain a balance between too much activity and too great a degree of lethargy. They may lack the intense drive and enthusiasms shown by high activity level writers but will be much better able to work methodically at the more routine tasks. They tend to be more tolerant of inactivity in others.

How You Will Relate to Them:

As your superior:

From an employee's viewpoint, a medium activity level superior is probably the easiest and most pleasant to work for. There will be none of the intense drive found in the high activity level superior, but they will still expect a reasonable output and performance, so you won't get a chance to feel boringly underoccupied. This type of individual is capable of working at pressure when the need arises, but sees no point in treating every activity as if it were an emergency. You will relate to such superiors well if your activity level is medium or on the low side, but if you are a high activity person then their reluctance to throw all their energies into every single task may prove irritating on occasions.

As your employee:

You will need to keep such a person busy in order to avoid a loss of motivation and interest in the job. But do not expect them to carry out strenuous or highly demanding work for extended periods. Such individuals will prefer to put in eight hours' work and then go home and forget about the job until the next day. They work best in occupations which involve a certain amount of routine interspersed with the stimulation provided by an occasional challenge or an unexpected change.

As your marriage partner:
They will enjoy a fairly settled domestic routine provided it is broken up with occasional changes to make life more interesting. Medium activity level people are prepared to do everyday chores but will tend to put off the bigger tasks – repairing a gutter, repainting the front door or mending a fence – for as long as possible. They will be happiest with partners who match them in activity levels, find the highly active too energetic and the very low activity partner too undemanding for their liking.

As your friend:
So far as most people are concerned this is the ideal activity level for a close friend. They will be energetic enough to enjoy occasional bursts of activity and you will not find them objecting bitterly to a proposed walk, a swimming trip or a game of tennis. But they will be equally contented lazing before a fire or watching TV. Unless your own activity level is very high or extremely low you should find a mutually satisfying friendship with such a person.

As your lover:
Unlike the high activity level lover they will be willing to indulge in romance and to enjoy a relaxing session of foreplay before love-making. During sex they will usually prove energetic and willing to try out different variations and experience new sorts of sexual activity. Unless your own activity level is extremely low or very high, middle activity lovers will prove the most satisfactory.

CATEGORY THREE – LOW ACTIVITY LEVEL

Pressure Guide

The writer can be placed in this category if their handwriting density matches lines *one or two* on the Intensity Index or if there are *five or less* sheets remaining on the Pressure Pad when the first, faint image is detected on the final sheet.

General Personality of Low Activity Writers

Such writers tend to avoid strenuous activities and to be rather lethargic in their approach to life. They will probably lack much enthusiasm or drive, even for pursuits and activities which really interest them. They prefer routine to change and the familiar to the unusual. The lower the scores on the tests (ie line one on the Intensity Index, only one or two sheets remaining on the Pressure Pad) the less energetic the writer is likely to prove.

How You Will Relate to Them:

As your superior:
They will tend to show little interest in what happens or how those working under them are doing their jobs. They are unlikely to put on much pressure or to assert much authority. Such writers are usually unwilling to drive themselves any harder than those who work under them. They will probably overdelegate and try to shift responsibility and blame to subordinates if things go wrong. A sudden crisis is almost certain to leave them unable to cope and they are best suited to work involving a familiar and secure routine. If you are a low activity level person yourself then such a superior should prove ideal. You will be left alone to get on with the tasks at your own pace, be free from constant pressure and never need to worry that something unexpected may happen to break the comfortable routine. Your superior will be just as anxious to avoid the unfamiliar as you are. On the debit side you may find yourself being unfairly criticised when things go wrong. If you are a medium to high activity level person then the attitude of such a superior will probably prove impossible to tolerate for any length of time. They will do their best to curb your enthusiasms by rejecting fresh ideas and frowning on too much expenditure of energy.

As your employee:
One might suppose that a low-activity-level person would be

the last man, or woman, you would want to employ. Certainly they are ill-suited to any position which requires them to work under pressure, to expend a lot of mental or physical energy or to cope with a sudden emergency. But there are many jobs where such an employee would prove ideal. If the work is routine and demands a methodical approach and an eye for detail then such a person may do extremely well. But do not expect them to show great enthusiasm for the work or to take much initiative in suggesting changes. In occupations where there is a high level of frustration, for example in a department which has to deal with complaints from the public but where there is a carefully laid down routine for dealing with such complaints, they are likely to prove more satisfactory than a high activity level employee. This is because, lacking great feelings of enthusiasm or interest for the job, they can remain objective about the critical comments and abuse.

As your marriage partner

No difficulties are likely to arise if you both have equally matched low activity levels. But such partners will rapidly irritate high activity level companions because of their lack of energy or enthusiasm for any proposed joint activities. They will be reluctant to exert themselves, even for a short time, and much prefer to stay at home. They are happiest in a settled routine or domestic lifestyle which makes no unexpected demands on them.

As your friend:

For a really satisfying friendship you will both need to have a low activity level. Even a medium activity level individual is likely to find the relationship so frustrating that it will soon be brought to an end.

As your lover:

As with friendship and marriage, low activity level people will find that lovers who share their disinclination for change and activity are most compatible. The submissive nature of this type of person sometimes appeals to those with a medium activity level who like to constantly dominate their sex companions although even they may soon grow irritated by their companions lack of enthusiasm or responsiveness. They will prefer sexual activities to follow a routine and prefer to avoid any changes, even in the time and place of their love-making.

Within each of these three categories you will find a range of activity levels. Some medium activity level writers, for example, may appear more like high or low level writers. The higher, or lower, the score on the pressure tests the more closely the writer is likely to match the personality sketches above.

Once the analysis of overall pressure has been completed, the next step is to move on to an examination of the way in which pressure has been applied when forming the strokes of different letters. This too has something very interesting and important to say about the writer concerned.

THE MEANING OF PRESSURE VARIATIONS

A careful study of the handwriting sample should reveal that some of the letter strokes have been formed with greater or lesser pressure than others. Bear in mind that the small, individual pen marks within a letter, for example the tail on the 'g', the curve on an 'o' or 'c' and the cross-bar on a 't' are produced in a split second of time. Such pressure variations within a single movement provide a very subtle indication of the writer's internal condition. There are two main sources of pressure variation that you will need to watch out for, cross-stroke pressure and random pressure patterns. Both offer valuable insights into the personality of the writer.

Cross-Stroke Pressure

In most normal handwriting, there is a distinctive pressure pattern which emphasises the downstrokes of the letters. This can be seen below where the arrows indicate pressure variations within the letter 'm'.

Fig. 13.

There is an increase in the force used for making the downward stroke (arrow 1) and a decrease on the upstroke (arrow 2). This ebb and flow of pressure and release which exists in the majority of handwriting samples produces a rhythmic pattern. Because this type of movement is the easiest and most natural to achieve, any departures from it are of special interest when making an analysis.

Cross-stroke pressure is one of the most frequently seen variations. Here the writer exerts additional force when making connecting strokes between letters, or when forming the cross-strokes of the 't', the 'f', and the capital 'H'.

This sideways pressure is illustrated below.

Fig. 14.

Look, first of all, at the connecting stroke which links the 'b' and the two 'o's in the word 'book' (indicated by arrow). The line is obviously darker and heavier indicating the use of extra pressure. This left-to-right increase is accompanied by a weakening of intensity within the 'o's themselves. It is often the case that additional sideways intensity in the letter strokes leads to a reduction of pressure on adjoining or nearby letters. Sideways pressure is also indicated in the words 'you' and 'in' by the arrows.

We have termed this sideways pressure 'goal motion', because it is normally found in writers who direct most of their energies towards specific goals, and are strongly achievement-motivated.

They will work with single-minded dedication towards whatever goals they have set themselves, and are not easily diverted. Such individuals need clear yardsticks by which to assess their successes. This may mean material rewards, high salaries or rapid promotion. But it could equally involve more abstract concepts of achievement, creating a work of art, playing a sport better or completing an intellectually demanding task. In his, or her, purposeful striving towards a target, such writers are likely to pay scant attention to areas of life which seem secondary to the chosen goal.

Sideways pressure can appear as a dominant trend or it may only be present here and there in the writing. If it is found only occasionally the writer will still possess the characteristics of behaviour we have described but to a lesser extent.

What can you expect when attempting to relate to such a person? As with overall pressure this depends on the nature of the relationship.

As your superior

Writers with lateral pressure will usually push both themselves and everybody else as hard as possible in order to achieve their goals. You may consider such a person your friend, but when the chips are down the need to achieve a certain goal is likely to override any considerations of friendship. You will rarely be able to get away with doing less than your fair share, even if you are on good terms outside the office. Such a person will seldom be content with second best and will see little merit in being a good loser. He or she is motivated to win and will attempt to do so with a single-mindedness of purpose which can be daunting to anybody less goal-orientated. If you see this sign in the handwriting of a prospective superior and want to enjoy an easy life – look for a different job!

As your employee

He or she will be largely self-motivated and work hard to complete projects. Such individuals can best be encouraged by offering tangible rewards for success, such as bonus payments, promotion and privileges, rather than praise alone. They will be single-minded and unlikely to allow sentiment or emotional considerations to divert them from a chosen goal. It is important not to over-motivate such people, however, especially if their handwriting also contains emotional disturbance or physical weakness (see chapters seven and eight for a detailed description of these indications). If the goals are seen as being too attractive, and the motivations offered are exceedingly powerful, there is a risk that such people will overstretch themselves and suffer a mental or physical collapse as a result. Watch the handwriting for signs of increased stress, using the technique described at the end of this chapter.

As your marriage partner
If the writer's goals are concerned with work, you may find yourself neglected. The need for achievement in this area will mean that home life, and marriage, plays a second best to the demands of the job. They will eagerly accept overtime and week-end work if it is likely to enhance their position. It is often hard for somebody married to such a single-minded individual to understand why they are unable to assume a larger role in their lives. When their goals are related to the home and family, you are liable to have little say in what decisions are taken. Once the goal-directed individual has made up his, or her, mind about the right course of action, it will be very hard to influence them. The most effective approach is likely to be one in which you get your way by diplomacy and tact.

As your friend
The goal-directed person often has little time for real friend-ships, unless they are in some way useful for furthering their chosen ends. Because of the single-mindedness shown by these individuals, relationships tend to get pushed into the back-ground. Do not be too surprised if arrangements to meet are cancelled at the last minute because 'something important has come up'. It will mean that a choice has had to be made between seeing you and something which might help in achieving an

important objective. In such a contest the friendship will always come a poor second.

As your lover

If an intimate relationship is the goal of this type of person then he, or she, will pursue this relationship with unwavering intensity. If the goals lie outside the relationship, however, then even the intimacy of the association is unlikely to save it should a goal-enhancing opportunity appear.

Random Pressure

Some handwriting reveals a pressure pattern which is irregular, with the density and thickness of strokes increasing and decreasing for no apparent reason. In the sample below, arrows indicated portions of the script where these fluctuations have occurred.

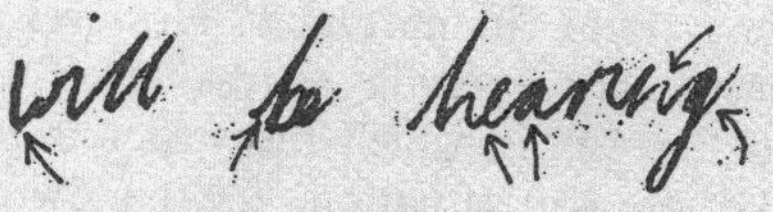

Fig. 15.

Random pressure can be related to a number of factors, but its underlying cause is the way in which commands from the motor-centres in the brain, which are responsible for directing all movements, reach the hand and fingers. Normally there should be a steady stream of electrical impulses to the writing muscles. Where random pressure is present, it is an indication that these signals are irregular and research has shown that this is often associated with emotional instability. Writers whose pressure is random will usually be more anxious than normal and prone to emotional upsets.

Random pressure is a general indication of these tendencies. But it cannot be used as a precise guide to the nature of the emotional disturbance. Use it as an initial signpost and go on to discover more detailed information, and confirmation of your original conclusion, by making use of the indicators described in chapter seven.

Sudden Sharp Pressure Increases

Random pressure can also be seen in the example below which contains, in addition, *sudden sharp increases* in pressure indicated by the arrows. Where such a sign appears it should be interpreted as an indication of instability, nervousness and a quick temper. Such writers are liable to fly off the handle all too easily and could become hostile and aggressive when frustrated.

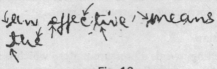

Fig. 16.

Handwriting Pressure and Everyday Stress Levels

An individual's handwriting pressure remains reasonably constant under normal circumstances. However there may be marked changes when everyday stress levels begin to rise. Depending on the way in which the writer is most likely to respond to the stressful situation, the handwriting pressure will either increase or decrease. By monitoring such fluctuations you can detect an unacceptable rise in the amount of stress you are under long before your body produces any more obvious, and serious, response. It is also possible to predict, again well in advance of the event, your probable reaction to such stress problems.

This is because, as we explained in chapter one, handwriting is such a sensitive indicator of the body's internal state. It might be likened to the recording device at an earthquake monitoring station. As external stresses increase they produce internal changes, the body's equivalent of an earth tremor, in the hormonal and nervous systems. Just as seismographic equipment is capable of detecting very small disturbances at a great distance, so too can the tip of the writing instrument transmit these bodily vibrations to the paper.

Pressure will either increase or decrease with rising stress levels depending on the writer's biological response to threatening or anxiety-producing situations. When these occur, we may either decide to stand and fight or turn and flee. The automatic defence system with which nature has equipped us ensures that, whatever choice we make, we have the best chance of surviving. But it does not make that decision for us. How we respond is determined by the higher reasoning processes and will be influenced by a whole range of factors, especially past experience.

There are two possible responses which enable us to classify stressful situations. There are Type E (Effort) Stresses which are so called because we are prepared to stay and fight, and Type F (Fear) Stresses which are likely to produce flight. We must make it clear that the difference lies not in the stresses themselves but in a particular individual's perception of them. Thus the same kind of stress, for example a confrontation with an aggressive boss, may be a Type E Stress situation for one person and a Type F Stress situation for another.

The different perceptions of a threat result in the body preparing itself to meet the difficulty in different ways. These differences are reflected in the nature of the handwriting pressure changes.

Type E (Effort) Stresses

Produce *increased* effort in response to the stressful situation. This is equivalent to the fight reaction. Muscle output rises in readiness to produce an intense release of effort. As a result the force used to overcome the resistance of the paper also increases and the pressure rises above the individual's normal baseline measure. The greater the increase in pressure the more Type E Stress is being experienced and the more probable it is that the writer intends to confront rather than avoid the situation.

Type F (Fear) Stresses

Produce *decreased* effort in response to the stressful situation. This is the fear and anxiety reaction. The individual is preparing for avoidance and escape. As this happens the major muscle groups, such as those in the shoulders, stomach area and limbs tense up. The extra energy invested in these parts of the body has to be drawn from somewhere and leads to a reduction in the amount of energy available for the secondary muscle groups, those involved in producing handwriting. The result is a noticeable decrease in overall handwriting pressure. The greater the decrease the more Type F stress is being experienced and the more likely it is that the person will decide that flight provides the best answer to the anxiety which the situation arouses.

It is important to realise that feelings of fear are often highly personal and subjective experiences. There are, of course, some situations which everybody with any sense would regard as a genuine threat to life and limb, an out-of-control car, a blazing building, a charging bull and so on. But, in other cases, the fears have no basis in reality and are acquired through inappropriate learning. For instance a spider phobic may show every sign of experiencing very real and intense terror when confronted by a small and harmless house spider. Equally the agoraphobic who is unable to walk down a street or the social phobic who experiences genuine fears about meeting people are responding to a response which has been learned. To the non-phobic all those experiences will seem perfectly normal and quite unalarming. For the phobic the fear is real enough but it is created by a particular attitude of mind, a way of looking at the world which is a result of that individual's previous experiences.

Because of this we cannot always tell when somebody else is experiencing rising stress levels and we may not always be able to detect such increases in our own lifestyle, especially at first when the rise is slight and there are few, if any, noticeable physical responses. We feel as relaxed as usual and seem to be able to cope with the demands of the situation as effectively as before. But, internally, adverse responses to the stressful conditions are starting to have an effect. They are slowly but surely undermining our mental and physical health. If caught in time it may be easy enough to make the appropriate changes and reorganise our lifestyles. Later on it could prove much harder to escape from the vicious downward spiral of increasing stress, producing a system which is less and less capable of handling it and so, inevitably, leading to an increase in stress.

You can check up on your own, or anybody else's, day-to-day stress responses by means of a simple handwriting test which takes only a few seconds to complete. Not only will it detect any rises in stress but it will also predict what sort of a response your body is preparing to make. Whether it is getting ready to respond with fight or flight. This can be extremely informative, even when you are monitoring your own behaviour. We often feel that we know exactly how we will react at the moment of truth. How we will handle any confrontation. We may, for example, be convinced that, when the time comes, we will be able to stand and fight. Or we might be equally certain that we will give up without a struggle and make any concessions in order to escape. These could be accurate perceptions. But there is often an element of self-deception about such predictions. We may cave in and reach almost any agreement that gets us off the hook even though, before the encounter, we had made up our minds to stand up for ourselves. On the other hand we may find it possible to put up a spirited defence which wins the day despite gloomy predictions of defeat.

To discover how you are most likely to react, make use of the Stress Barometer described below.

THE STRESS BAROMETER

A step-by-step guide to constructing this handwriting stress barometer is shown below (Figure 17). The Barometer should be produced at a time when the writer is not under any special stress or pressure. Perhaps in the evening or after a relaxing weekend.

Write using a biro and imagine that you are sending a note to a friend when forming the first (N) line. When creating the lightest line pressure your pen should just glide over the surface of the paper.

Once the Barometer has been constructed keep it in a safe place and make use of the scales any time you want to check your stress level and most likely response to a current difficulty. To do this simply use two pieces of paper and a sheet of carbon as you did before. Write the same sentence, once only, in your normal handwriting pressure. Compare the second copy with the Barometer.

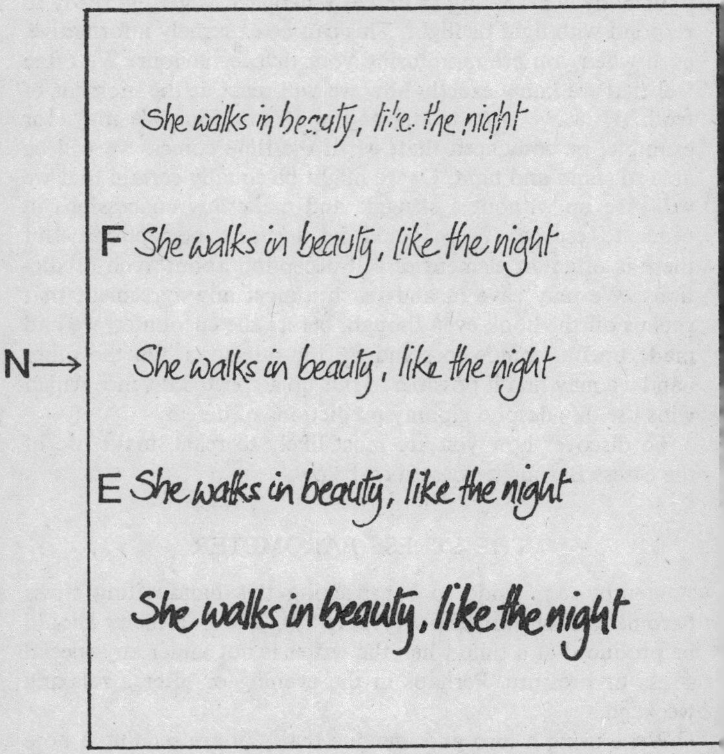

She walks in beauty, like the night

F She walks in beauty, like the night

N→ She walks in beauty, like the night

E She walks in beauty, like the night

She walks in beauty, like the night

Fig. 17.

Constructing The Stress Barometer

Step One
Take two sheets of paper and place a sheet of carbon between them.

Step Two
Write a few words using biro and *normal* pressure. Pretend you are writing a line to a friend. Against this line write the letter 'N'.

Step Three
At the bottom of the page repeat the line using *as much pressure as possible* without actually tearing the paper.

Step Four
Between the two lines repeat the words a third time. Now try to use a pressure which is approximately half-way between your normal and heaviest pressure. Against this line write a capital 'E'. This is the 'Effort' warning level of handwriting pressure.

Step Five
At the top of the sheet write the line yet again using the *lightest* possible pressure which will still leave a mark on the paper.

Step Six
Finally, between the top and middle lines write the same words using a pressure which is half-way between the lightest and the normal pressure used. Against this line write the capital letter 'F'. This is the 'Fear' warning level of handwriting pressure.

Step Seven
Discard the top copy and keep the bottom one which will show greater contrast. To use the Barometer at another time, repeat steps one and two, copy out the same line using new sheets of white and carbon paper. Compare the bottom copy

with your Barometer and notice which lines come closest in pressure.

now is the time for all	*Line One:* Ultra-light pressure. Used for construction purposes only. Not needed when comparing samples.
F now is the time for all	*Line Two:* Light pressure. Represents a stress danger level. Predicts flight as the most likely response.
now is the time for all	*Line Three:* Normal pressure. A comparison line. Any substantial increase or decrease in subsequent samples indicates a change in stress levels.
E now is the time for all	*Line Four:* Heavy pressure. Represents a stress danger level. Predicts fight as the most likely response.
now is the time for all	*Line Five:* Ultra-heavy pressure. Used for construction purposes only. Not needed when comparing samples.

If your handwriting pressure has remained the same, it will match that of the middle line (marked N for normal) on the Monitor. This means that you are not experiencing any greater stress than you were when you constructed the Barometer.

Substantial changes in handwriting pressure, as it appears on the new sample, indicate an increase in stress levels by comparison with the normal period when the Barometer was constructed.

The two lines to check on the Barometer are those marked 'E' and 'F'. A major change in pressure indicates rising stress. If your pressure is as light or lighter than the 'F' (Fear) line it indicates that your system is preparing to meet a stressful situation with avoidance and flight.

If your pressure is as dark or darker than the 'E' (Effort) line it means that you are preparing to stand and fight.

You should consider the 'E' and 'F' lines as danger levels. If the handwriting pressure on your sample is lighter than the 'F' line or darker than the 'E' line, then you are experiencing an unacceptably high level of stress. You should take prompt steps to rectify matters. Try to reduce the number of demands being made on you, take more time off and develop interests which help you to relax and unwind.

It is a good idea to keep a regular check on your stress levels, even if life does not seem to be especially stressful just at the moment. Stresses can all too easily build up and catch one unawares. If you are going through a particularly busy or difficult and demanding period of life then a weekly or even a daily stress check would be a worthwhile idea. Once the Barometer is constructed it will take you only a few seconds to write the stress check sentence and make the comparisons.

The piece of handwriting which we asked you to produce at the end of the last chapter can be used at this point to assess some of the pressure indications in your own writing. Use the Intensity Index to obtain an estimate of overall pressure and study the script to see if there is any evidence of cross-stroke pressure or irregular pressure patterns. But, once you have done this, keep the sample. We have only just begun to describe the wealth of insights which can be obtained from handwriting's hidden language.

Chapter Four

The Meaning of Movement and Flow

Handwriting may be analysed not only for the pressure but also the pace, that is the speed and flow, of word formation. Speed simply means the rate at which the pen is moved across the paper. Flow refers to the freedom of movement used when shaping the letters and words. Both have a great deal to tell us about the writer and are second only in importance to pressure as a basis for analysing handwriting.

We will explain exactly what movement and flow reveal about a writer's intelligence and personality, and how you can interpret them correctly, in a moment. But before you read any further in this chapter please carry out the following check on your own handwriting.

THE HANDWRITING SPEED TEST

You will need a watch with a sweep second hand, a digital watch or, best of all, a stop-watch; a sheet of unlined paper and whatever sort of pen you normally write with.

Start by memorising the short sentence below so that you can write it down without pausing to reflect or to consult the book. Write the sentence exactly as it is printed here. Do *not* start with a capital 'L' or finish with a full-stop.

look while your hand moves along the page

When the eight words are fixed in your mind, prepare to time yourself writing them down. If you have a stop-watch hold it ready in your non-writing hand. If you are using an ordinary watch set it on the table before you so that the dial can easily be seen, and begin writing as the second hand reaches twelve. If you are using a digital watch it is easiest to begin when the seconds show zero.

As soon as you have stopped writing, note the time. When using a wristwatch it is possible to obtain a more precise estimate, which tends to eliminate variations in starting and stopping the timing, by taking an average. Probably the easiest way of doing this, if you like to keep your sums simple, is to take five readings, total them up and divide by five to obtain the average time.

In order to get the most value from this check you should carry it out before reading any further. A more accurate result will be obtained if you are not aware, at this point, of exactly what is being assessed.

WHAT THE HANDWRITING SPEED TEST TELLS YOU

The sentence you were asked to write was specially devised so as to be fairly short, easy to remember and containing a fair number of ascenders (letters like 'l', 'k' and 't' whose stroke rises above the writing line) and descenders (letters like 'p', 'q', and 'y' whose stroke falls below the writing line).

As part of our researches into the relationship between handwriting and personality, we asked a large number of people – of different ages and from different occupations – to write that sentence. They were then given other psychological tests and the results analysed statistically. This enabled us to draw up the Comparison Chart shown below.

Handwriting speed is important because studies have shown a link between it and verbal abilities. The faster a person writes the more articulate they are likely to prove. By checking your own speed against the Chart you can discover where you stand in relation to the rest of the population. This, in turn, will allow you to compare yourself to others on verbal effectiveness.

Speed Test Chart

Handwriting Speed in Seconds	12	13	14	15	16	17	18	19	20	21
Percentage of people who are faster than you when writing	% 10	% 15	% 23	% 30	% 40	% 50	% 60	% 70	% 77	% 85
Percentage of people who are slower than you when writing	% 90	% 85	% 77	% 70	% 60	% 50	% 40	% 30	% 23	% 15

Handwriting Speed and Word Power

If you wrote those eight words in 15 *seconds or less*, consider yourself as having a superior writing speed. This probably means that you are also skilled in the use of words, talk fluently and have an above-average vocabulary. It is likely that you enjoy playing around with words, for instance inventing rhymes and thinking up verbal jokes such as puns. People with a high verbal ability are good with any task which requires a manipulation of words, and they can usually learn new languages without difficulty. They have an above-average understanding of written material and are able to remember more of what they read.

It is important to bear in mind, however, that handwriting speed alone is not a *test* of verbal ability. It is a factor which has been found to be closely associated with word skills.

Word Power and IQ

Alfred Binet, the father of the modern IQ test, was firmly convinced that handwriting could be used to assess intelligence. As long ago as 1909 he was working on techniques for relating handwriting to IQ. Binet never published his findings, however, and they were lost after his death.

In recent years there has been a strong renewal of interest in the relationship between a person's level of intelligence and the way in which he writes. Research by experimental psychologists in America and Europe has shown that not only is handwriting analysis a very reliable method of assessing IQ, but also one of the simplest available.

Verbal ability is one component of what psychologists term *general intelligence*. This also includes such mental skills as problem-solving, abstract reasoning and number manipulation. So handwriting speed alone can only provide partial information on a person's intelligence. In order to obtain an overall picture of that individual's total intellectual capacity, we must consider *not only how fast he writes but how the faster speeds are achieved*.

Intelligent writers simplify their letter forms in various ways which involve departures from the writing style taught at school. By using an economical style of writing which eliminates unnecessary strokes the writer can achieve a considerable saving of time, thus achieving a more rapid writing speed. The more subtle, numerous and efficient these alterations the higher the IQ of the writer.

One of the most important studies of handwriting simplifications and IQ was carried out by Dr. Peter Castelnuovo-Tedesco, now Head of the Department of Psychiatry at Harbor General Hospital, Torrance, California. He found that not only was it possible to predict intelligence very accurately in this way but that people with no knowledge of psychology were able to obtain reliable assessments after only a few minutes' instruction.

HOW TO STUDY SIMPLIFICATIONS

The kind of simplifications commonly found in the handwriting of people with above-average education and intelligence can best be described by illustrations of actual samples taken from our case files.

Example One

The most common form of simplification occurs with the elimination of upper and lower letter loops. These can be seen

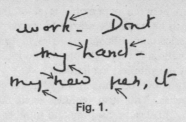

Fig. 1.

arrowed in the sample. This is a slight but important departure from the style of writing taught in school and a preliminary indication that the writer may be of above-average intelligence. A really bright writer will, however, use many more simplifications, some of which are highly original and clever.

Example Two

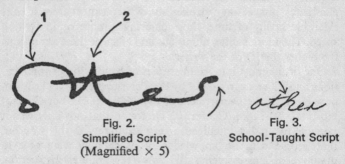

Fig. 2.
Simplified Script
(Magnified × 5)

Fig. 3.
School-Taught Script

The word 'other' has been magnified in this example to make the important simplifications easier to see. Arrow 1 draws attention to the connection between the 'o' and the 't'. Compare this with the school-taught model of the word. Notice the economy of movement in the simplified version. The letters are formed and joined with a minimum of stroke effort. Arrow 2 indicates a similar saving of time in the formation of the 'th' shape. Notice how the letters are produced by three simple movements, a rhythmic down, up, down, stroke of the pen. Compare this with the school-taught form of 'th' shown by Figure 3.

Finally observe the letter 'r'. This has been written with great economy yet still remains legible. Here again a comparison with the school-taught version of the letter is instructive.

Example Three

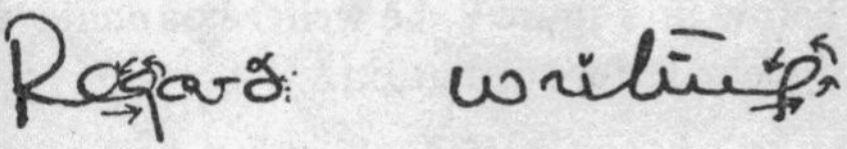

Fig. 4.
Simplified Form of 'g'

Fig. 5.
Standard Form of 'g'

The letter 'g' in the words 'Regard' and 'writing' is made with a rapid movement which is the reverse of that taught at school. This saves the writer a small but significant amount of time because the letter can be formed in a fluid movement, as shown by the arrows. They also show how the pen moves in each case as the letters are written, and provide a comparison between the simplified 'g' and the standard 'g'. The simplified 'g' is still perfectly legible.

Example Four

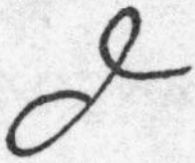

Fig. 6.
Simplied letter 'd'

Fig. 7.
Standard letter 'd'

Here the 'd' has been formed with an elevated loop which is the complete opposite of the downward directed loop taught in schools. The writer has made a direct connection between the elevated loop and the adjoining letter. The simplifications described here and in Example Three have been shown by Dr. Lawrence Epstein and his associates at New York University to be indicative of an above-average level of education, which is in turn an indication of greater intellectual abilities.

A word of caution about simplifications seems advisable at this point. You should not confuse *artfully simplified* writing with *neglected writing*. That is, the deviations from copybook letter formation must not have occurred at the expense of legibility. As we said earlier speed alone is *not* the crucial factor. There must be a combination of speed and clear letter formation.

The difference between artful simplification and neglect can be seen in the samples below. In Figure 9 the writer has achieved speed at the expense of clear letter formation.

your individual

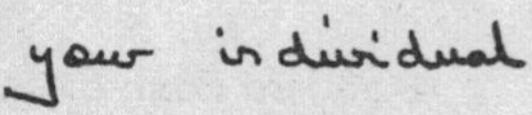

Fig. 8.
Artfully Simplified
Writing

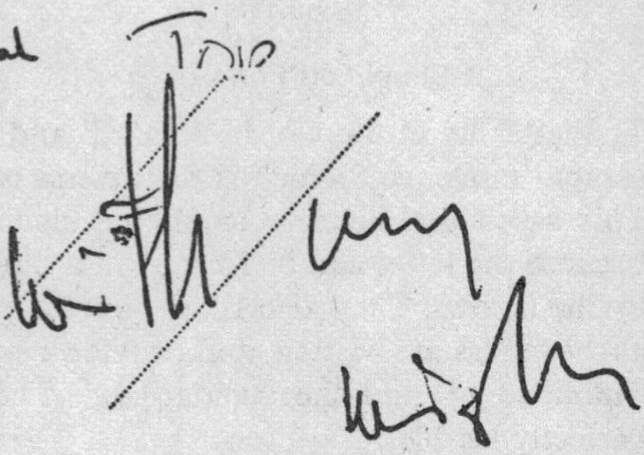

Fig. 9.
Neglected Writing

GIVING YOUR HANDWRITING AN IQ TEST

The five examples of handwriting below show gradually increasing levels of simplification. The first illustrates a type of writing very close to that taught at school. The second example contains some basic simplifications, while the third has a moderately high level of simplification. In four and five we can see a much greater degree of simplification which indicates that the writers are at the highest levels of intelligence.

To give your handwriting the IQ test compare the sample which you prepared at the end of chapter two with these examples. Notice the number and type of simplifications which you have employed and decide which of the five levels shown applies to your own writing. Once you have made the comparison, find out your general intelligence and sort of occupation in which you are best suited by referring to the chart below. But before doing so we suggest that you read our comments on the relationship between general intelligence levels and occupational success.

Handwriting IQ Comparisons

Sample Number

One

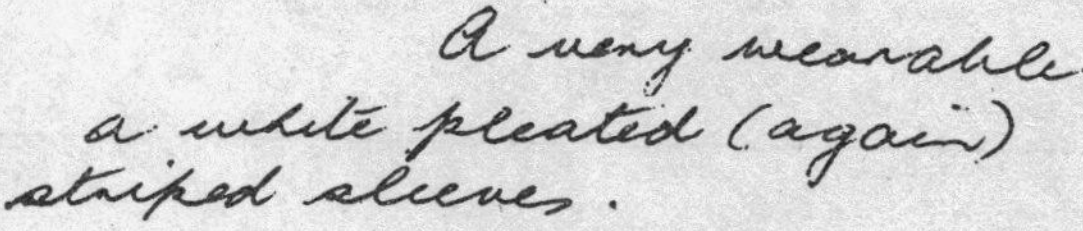

A very wearable
a white pleated (again)
striped sleeves.

Fig. 10.

Two

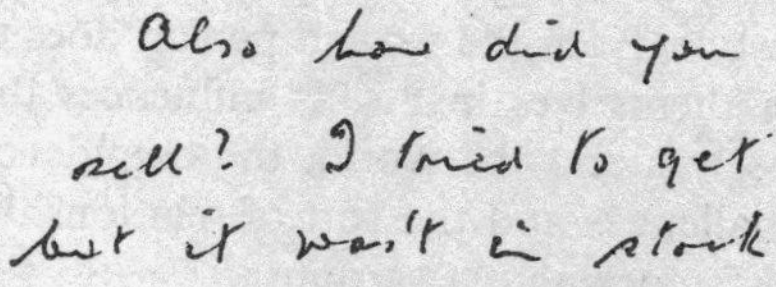

Also how did you
sell? I tried to get
but it wasn't in stock

Fig. 11.

Three

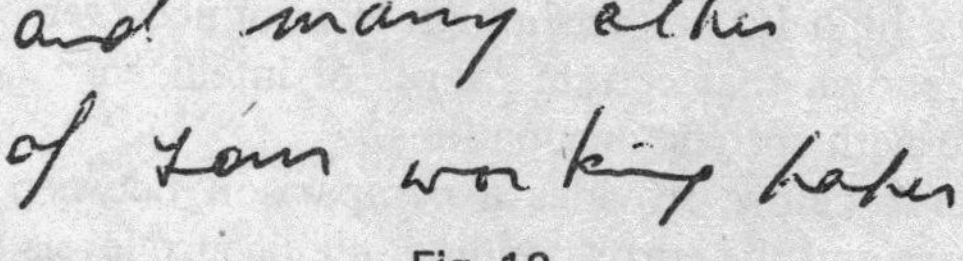

and many other
of I am working harder

Fig. 12.

Four

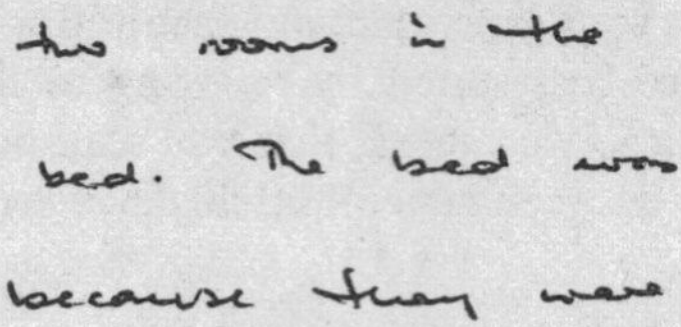

two rooms in the

bed. The bed was

because they were

Fig. 13.

Five

or it would

This week could

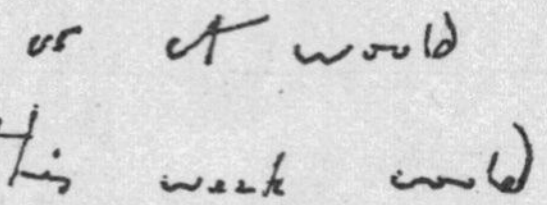

Fig. 14.

IQ AND THE JOBS WE DO

Research has shown that intelligence is not only related to success in school or college. It has a profound effect on many aspects of lifestyle, from the work a person does to the kind of goals they set themselves in life. It influences the image they have of themselves and the world, the confidence with which they tackle challenges and the sort of relationships which they find most satisfactory and rewarding.

A common mistake, however, is to believe that the higher a person's IQ the better all these aspects of living will be. This is often very far from true and is nowhere better illustrated than by considering job satisfaction and success. It is simply not the case that a high IQ predicts a high level of achievement, but it has been shown that certain ranges of intelligence *tend* to be associated with specific occupations.

The chart below provides a comparison between different occupations and the corresponding intelligence levels expressed in terms of the handwriting simplifications illustrated above. The information is based on data from a wide range of studies.

Handwriting and Intelligence Chart

Number of Example which matched your handwriting.	Level of Intelligence Indicated.	Type of Occupation likely to prove most appropriate.
One	Average	Barber, cook, auto mechanic, truck driver, welder, butcher, lumberjack, farmer, miner, clerical worker, bartender, shop assistant, builder, machine operator.
Two	Above Average	Fireman, policeman, clerk, radio or TV repairman, salesman, commercial artist, retail store manager, watchmaker, sales assistant, tool-maker, machinist.
Three	Considerably Intelligent	Journalist, teacher, pharmacist, book-keeper, sales manager, photographer, short-hand secretary, politician, computer programmer.
Four	Highly Intelligent	Accountant, publisher, lawyer, doctor, engineer, business executive, airline pilot, architect, university lecturer.

Number of Example which matched your handwriting.	Level of Intelligence Indicated.	Type of Occupation likely to prove most appropriate.
Five	Extremely Intelligent	Philosopher, university professor, theoretical mathematician, physicist, high-level research scientist, computer systems analyst.

It is important to grasp that the Chart is not meant to suggest that people who have one of the jobs listed against the different styles of handwriting will invariably write in exactly that way. What it does mean is that, where the writer uses the degree of simplification illustrated by a particular example, their intellectual capacity should be equal to the demand of the occupation listed. They would be able to cope with such a career and find within it the mental stimulation likely to result in enjoyment and success.

Simplifications develop in the handwriting as we mature intellectually and are usually fully evolved by the late 'teens. They can, therefore, be used as a method for estimating the likely intellectual potential of a school-leaver if one is asked to provide career guidance. They also offer a trouble-free method for monitoring a child's mental development. The handwriting of a youngster which reveals intelligent simplifications at an early age indicates a faster than average rate of intellectual growth. They are especially significant when found in children under the age of twelve.

It is very likely that these youngsters will already show a preference for mentally-taxing and stimulating activities. They should certainly be encouraged in these interests and given every opportunity to further develop their minds. Some of the ways in which this can be achieved are explained in a soon-to-be published book by one of the authors (David Lewis)*. If you intend to use handwriting analysis to assess the IQ of children and adolescents it is essential to bear two points in mind.

Contrary to popular belief, intellectual abilities are not inborn and invariable. They are highly dependent on a whole range of factors relating to the individual's perceptions and lifestyle. Self-image and the way in which the youngster is regarded by important adults, such as parents and teachers, plays a crucial role. No less important are opportunities and motivations, encouragement and help, the example set by other members of the family and the attitudes of parents towards intelligent behaviour.

No one should *ever* be categorised as stupid on the basis of any single assessment, whether this involves an analysis of handwriting or the administration of an IQ test. Once categorised in this way there is a grave danger of creating a self-fulfilling prophecy.

The second thing to remember is that intelligence is only one component of success in life. Personality is just as vital and, in many instances, may prove a more powerful factor in achievement. Given the choice between employing somebody with a high IQ and an unpleasant personality or a person with a somewhat lower IQ who is easy to work with, most bosses will have no hesitation in choosing the latter. Personality also affects relationships and the individual who has the knack of getting on well with others may find promotion comes far more quickly.

We have already looked at some of the ways in which handwriting can be used to discover aspects of the writer's personality. In chapter one we considered the meaning of anchor strokes and missing 'i' dots. Activity levels, discussed in the previous chapter, are also related to personality. Now we want to describe two other important aspects of an individual's personality which is revealed in the appearance of the writing.

* *You Can Teach Your Child Intelligence* – Souvenir Press.

HOW DOES YOUR HANDWRITING FLOW?

The flow factor in writing was first investigated by the internationally renowned German psychiatrist and neurologist Dr. Rudolf Pophal. His extensive research established two aspects of handwriting flow which have a direct bearing on personality. These have been called *release* and *restraint*.

Restrained Writing

Although the samples of handwriting below differ in size, slant and style they have one basic and important characteristic in common – they are extremely rigid. Their appearance is stiff and monotonous, like a parade ground full of guardsmen at attention.

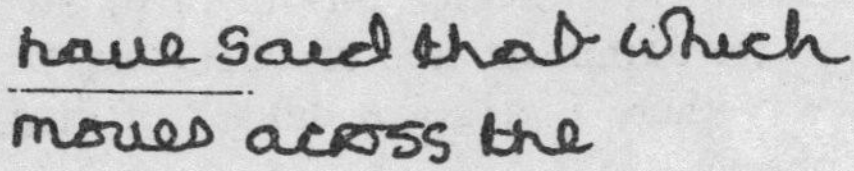

have said that which
moves across the

Fig. 15.

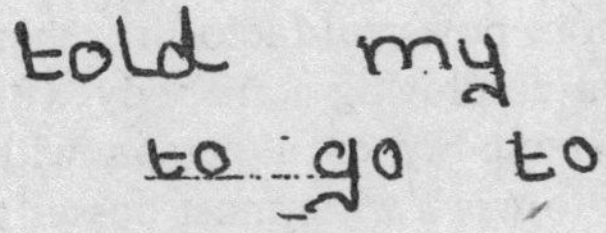

told my attemptal to
to go to several

Fig. 16. 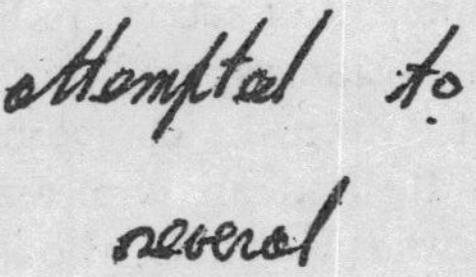   Fig. 17.

Tautness is apparent in the writing muscles as the forward movement of the pen is carefully restrained. The rigidity of the strokes restricts the writer's ability to form words and sentences in one smooth flow of movement. Study these examples carefully because they provide clear illustrations of extreme rigidity. Any writing you come across which exhibits these characteristics has been produced by a restrained personality.

Released Writing

Compare the style of the restrained writer with the examples below. Here the writing impulse is unbroken and the words sweep forward.

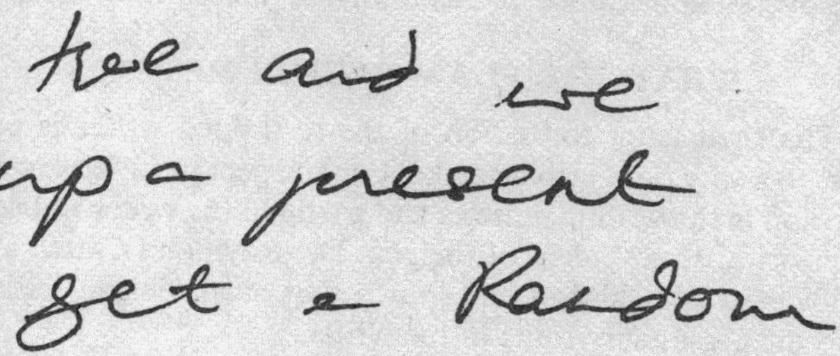

Fig. 18.

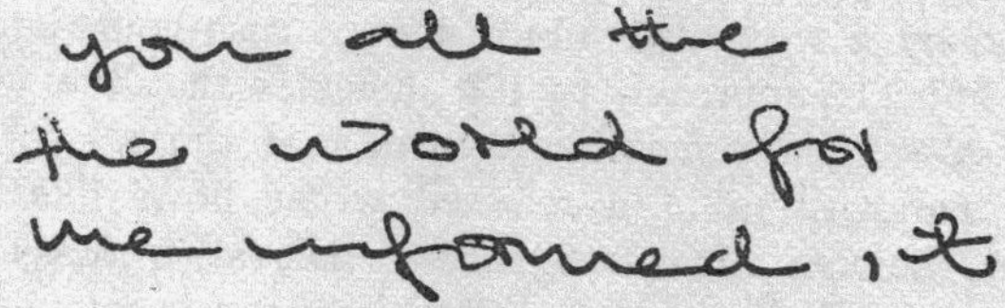

Fig. 19.

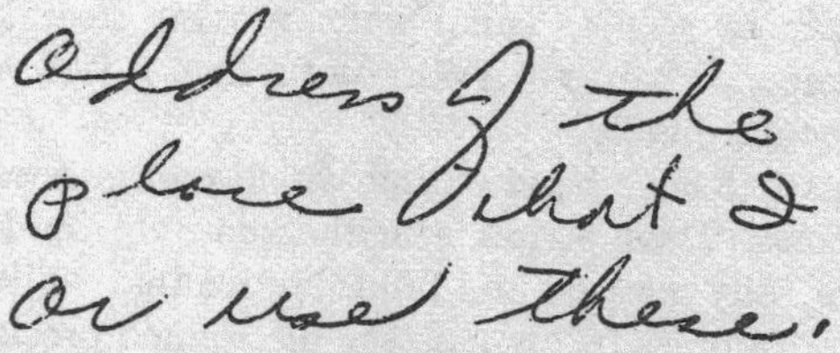

Fig. 20.

Examples of Released Writing

There is a certain amount of sloppiness in the letter formation because less effort has been made to control the pen. But even where there are broken connections, the writing motion continues forward in a smooth flow. The words have a fluency and a vitality. Compared to the granite-carved letters of the rigid writer they are formed from quicksilver.

A restrained writer concentrates on letter formation even

though his handwriting may not be very legible. The released writer regards freedom of movement as more important than the overall appearance of each individual letter and word.

WHAT THE FLOW FACTOR REVEALS

The rigid letter formation of the restrained writer is partly due to a very tight grip being kept on the pen, partly to excessive tension in the writing muscles and partly to the writer restricting the forward movement of the pen. Dr. Raymond Cattell at the University of Chicago has shown that such tension indicates specific personality traits in the writer.

The firm grip on the pen has something in common with the clenching of teeth to suppress anger or the tight grip on the steering by a frustrated motorist in a rush-hour jam. This white knuckle approach to life indicates that the writer is deeply concerned to maintain control at all times.

The handwriting of a released writer flows like a river towards the ocean. It is free, unrestricted, rather messy around the edges and likely to cause difficulties if it gets completely out of control. The restricted writer's script, using the same comparison, can be seen as canal water moving steadily between firmly channelled banks in a purposeful line. It is never allowed to flow uncontrollably.

Many people have handwriting which comes between these two extremes. Their script is neither entirely rigid and controlled nor fully released and fluid. Notice that while the letter strokes in examples below lack the disciplined precision of the

Fig. 21.

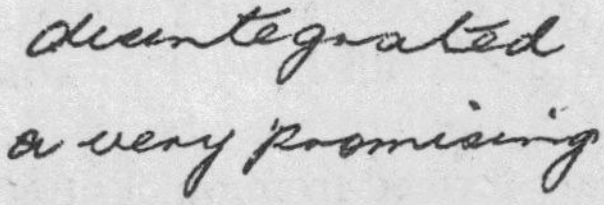

Fig. 22.

fully restrained writer they have not achieved the effortless flow which is found in released writing. The writer carefully maintains a style which achieves a middle ground between complete freedom and total control. This reflects a desire to avoid extremes which is also likely to reveal itself in other aspects of the individual's approach to life. These writers tend to adopt either a controlled and conformist attitude or, equally, may choose to follow a freer, less conformist lifestyle. Which course is adopted will very much depend on the circumstances and is never likely to be as extreme as the fully restrained or the completely released writer. Such individuals are flexible and can adapt themselves to the demands of a particular situation in a way which either of the other type of writers would find almost impossible.

By analysing the flow factor you can make a very rapid, but generally reliable, estimation of the writer's personality and approach to life. Rigid writers seek to control both their own lives and those around them, and they dislike any situation which robs them of this ability to exert their influence on events. The released writer is concerned with enjoying liberated relationships and in exploring feelings in order to extend and understand his, or her, own personality. Handwriting which comes between the two extremes reflects a middle-of-the-road approach with the characteristics of either type present to a lesser extent.

Clearly the different styles of writing predict very different responses to the problems and challenges of life. What can you expect from each of the extremes in different relationships?

As before we will examine these possible interactions under the five main headings of employer and employee, marriage partner, friend and lover.

As your superior:

Restrained Writers

They will be cautious and conformist; dress and behaviour will be very conventional. They are worriers who want to establish as much control as possible in their working environments. This will include attempts to control their employees which may lead to undue interference and unnecessary supervision. Their moods are fairly even and predictable, although if control does snap there may be a strong outburst of anger and frustration.

Released Writers

Generally easy-going and less conformist than the restrained writer. Even if the demands of the job require conventional dress they will secretly yearn to be wearing casual, individualistic clothes and to kick over the traces. They will be fascinated by new ideas, by the unusual and the unfamiliar. Routine will be tiresome for them and they will not become over-anxious about the occasional loss of control. They may be moody and will not mind revealing their feelings to subordinates.

As your employee:

Restrained Writers

They are likely to be conventional, cautious, and unwilling to take risks which might result in a loss of control. They tend to worry about such things as promotion, responsibilities and what their boss and colleagues think of them. They will conceal their true emotions so it is hard to know exactly how they are reacting to their working life. They will be even-tempered and more dependable than the released writer. They have greater powers of concentration and are especially good at work which requires attention to detail. They will tend to dislike tasks where there is the risk of things getting out of hand.

Released Writers

Do not offer them assignments which require a 'by the rule book' approach. They are best suited to tasks requiring imagination and creativity, where the end is more important than the means. They will find it hard to work under a rigidly conformist employer who will undoubtedly find them just as difficult to understand. They are not likely to worry much about small points of detail provided the overall appearance is satisfactory. They are less persistent and more easily distracted than most.

As your marriage partner:

Restrained Writers

A match between a restrained and a released writer is likely to be difficult. Their personalities will be so different as to produce many clashes and rows. The restrained writer will try to control most aspects of the marriage including the sharing of emotions. They will find it very hard to express their deepest feelings and will tend to bottle up hurt feelings and wounded pride. At times of marital crisis restrained writers will attempt to detach themselves from the situation by intellectualising the problems. That is, they will refuse to apply any subjective judgements and attempt to turn the problem into an academic exercise, simply because this gives them a greater feeling of control. They are unlikely to be moody, but will show occasional outbursts of anger or misery.

Released Writers

Their 'live for today and let tomorrow take care of itself' philosophy will probably upset a more conservative partner. So too may their impulsivity which often leads them to blurt things out with little thought for the consequences. Released writers express their emotions easily and these are liable to fluctuate between moods of elation and depression. Since they are less persistent and more easily distracted than other people, released writers may give in to a partner's wishes simply because they lose interest in the subject. The unfamiliar holds a great attraction for them and they love novelty and changes.

As your friend:

Restrained Writers

They tend to have a fairly small number of friends but to value them highly and work at maintaining the relationships. They will not enjoy emotional scenes or doing something unexpected.

Do not spring a surprise party or invitation on them because they may be embarrassed and uncomfortable at the resulting loss of control. Do not be surprised if they seem to take upsets without much outward expression of feelings. As we have already explained, they tend to bottle up their emotions, sometimes to an unnatural extent.

Released Writers

They will often have a large number of friendships maintained at a fairly superficial level. At a party the released writer usually spends a small amount of time with a great number of people, rather than monopolising any one guest for the whole evening. This can be seen less as a desire to be very friendly and more as a need for regular stimulation. If they have to maintain an uncomfortable level of control in their jobs, being with a group allows them to temporarily relinquish this control and give vent to their impulsive natures.

They can be moody and unpredictable, and they will prefer to do things on the spur of the moment rather than carefully plan them. Emotional scenes are not uncommon, because of their fluctuating moods and the lack of restraint with which their feelings are expressed. But you should not take such scenes too seriously. They will probably be forgotten completely a few hours later.

As your lover:

Restrained Writers

The restrained writer's preference for conformity may lead to a certain amount of anxiety about an intimate relationship which is in any way unconventional. The amount of guilt associated with the liaison is likely to be a direct reflection of the attitudes of those around them. If the community in which they live and work stresses the sanctity of marriage and the wickedness of 'living in sin' then they are liable to be very anxious and uncomfortable in such a relationship. If the atmosphere is relaxed and tolerant they may actually enjoy 'conforming' to the nonconformity of those around them.

They are unlikely to express their deep-felt emotions and may even give the appearance of not especially valuing the relationship. But they are capable of intense feelings and, in the long term, may prove more constant lovers than the mercurial released writer.

Released Writers

They relish unconventional relationships which help them to express their individuality. But they may not take them very seriously and as a result can unintentionally hurt a more deeply involved partner. They are not too concerned about what others think and will make little attempt to conceal their relationships. Because they are impulsive they may speak without thinking and then regret it later. If this happens, they will play up to their partner in a flirtatious way in order to get back into favour. Since they are capable of expressing emotions very freely, they will not mind if their partner does the same. But the moods they show are often rather superficial and can change readily, fluctuating readily between elation and despondency. They look to their partner as a source of stability in their lives and one of their greatest fears is the loss of that support.

As you can see, a knowledge of the flow factor provides a substantial amount of information about a writer. When this is combined with an ability to interpret pressure and its variation, you have taken a major first step towards understanding others through an analysis of their handwriting. In later chapters we shall be explaining how you can focus in on specific details of the script in order to gain even greater insights.

But what happens if the only example of a person's handwriting which you have is a signature, perhaps scrawled, at the bottom of a typewritten page! In fact this is often the *only* sample of handwriting which you are able to obtain. Can anything about the writer's character be discovered from such an apparently trivial source of information? The answer is – yes a great deal! In the next chapter we will be explaining exactly what we really say every time we sign our names.

Chapter Five

The Secret Meaning of Your Signature

Your name may be the most indiscreet thing you ever write. Although few people ever realise the fact, their signature is one-line autobiography with an intimate and truthful tale to tell. It reveals how you see the world and how you would like to be regarded by other people. It discloses details of your social attitudes and personal ambitions. It contains clues about your strengths and your weaknesses.

To those who have learned how to interpret the secret meaning of signatures, every one is a fascinating pen portrait of the writer. Once you have mastered the skill it is possible to discover how that person would relate to you as a friend or a marriage partner, an employer or a lover. In fact there are few important details about ourselves which we do not betray during the seemingly innocent act of signing our names.

A signature is not just another piece of handwriting, because names have an importance which puts them in a class of their own. Ask the average person – 'Who are you?' and they will most probably reply with their names. This happens so frequently and appears such a natural thing to do that we never give it a second thought. Indeed the normal response is to give your own name in exchange.

But consider the implications of this automatic answer. It means that names are not merely a convenient label used to identify the speaker, *they are that person*! If identification was their only function then numbers would do the job far more efficiently because everybody could be given a different code. There would be none of the confusions which arise through people sharing identical names. Yet we rebel at the very thought. The idea of being a number, rather than having a name, seems so impersonal that we usually adopt the procedure only when there is a deliberate intention to dehumanise, for example by giving convicted prisoners numbers in place of their names. The harsher the prison régime, and the greater the desire to destroy any sense of individuality among the inmates, the more strictly the 'numbers only' regulation will be applied.

The key significance of names is reflected in social customs and rituals in every culture. In some primitive tribes a child is not even regarded as having an existence until given a name. In the West it is not only the deeply religious who regard baptism as a ceremony of special importance. During a wedding, the marriage bond is symbolised by the woman 'giving up' her name for that of the husband. In some parts of the world, people believe that to know a person's name is to obtain some magical hold over them. Our own language recognises the value of the name in such comments as 'having a good name', 'giving a dog a bad name', and of carrying on the traditions of a 'proud name'.

It is not just a question of how we feel about our own names. The way other people regard us, at least when first introduced, is often heavily influenced by our names. Strong names – James, Michael, Kate and Susan for instance – tend to convey a sense of forthright determination. Softer names – such as Cecil, Paul, Daphne and Cloe – have a more passive, submissive quality to them. Actors, actresses and writers recognise the value of having the 'right name' for the kind of image they wish to project to the public and seldom present themselves with the 'unsuitable' names given by their parents. Finally we can identify the different roles within a relationship by the way in which names are used, from the very formal greeting to a superior by a subordinate – in which the name may be replaced by some status-bestowing title such as 'Sir' or 'Madam' – to an intimate encounter between old friends where names may be shortened or changed to emphasise the familiarity of the relationship, James becoming Jim, Catherine changing to Kate or the actual name being replaced by some nickname known only to close associates.

The value we give to names means that our signature,

perhaps more than any other single piece of writing, comes to be a vivid expression of the way we see ourselves and expect others to see us.

WHAT OUR SIGNATURE REALLY SAYS

The most dramatic way of illustrating the amount of information which can be gleaned from a person's signature is by describing two actual case histories taken from our files. Both deal with interpretations made for the purpose of advising on employment problems. But exactly the same techniques can, of course, be applied to the analysis of signatures for any purpose.

Case History One - The Agitated Art Director

Sally, a thirty-year-old art director with an American advertising agency, came to us for advice at what seemed to be a major turning point in her career. She had been with the same company for six years, was highly thought of by her employers and related well to her immediate superior. Word of her creative talent had got around and she found herself approached by a prestigious New York agency. The salary was better, the company had an international reputation and the prospects for promotion seemed excellent. Naturally Sally was tempted and being encouraged by her husband, who was also in advertising, to accept the offer. But Sally hesitated. The cause of her agitation was the fact that, during her interview, she had formed a very negative impression of the man who would be her superior in the agency. She had come away with the feeling that their working relationship might be difficult. Now she wanted to find out if there was anything in his handwriting which would provide insights into his personality. The only sample available was his signature, see Figure 1, at the bottom of a typewritten letter. After analysing the handwriting we advised Sally to turn down the offer despite its apparent attractions. What led us to this suggestion? We felt that there were clear indications in the signature that Sally would find it almost impossible to work closely and agreeably with such an individual.

Yours sincerely,

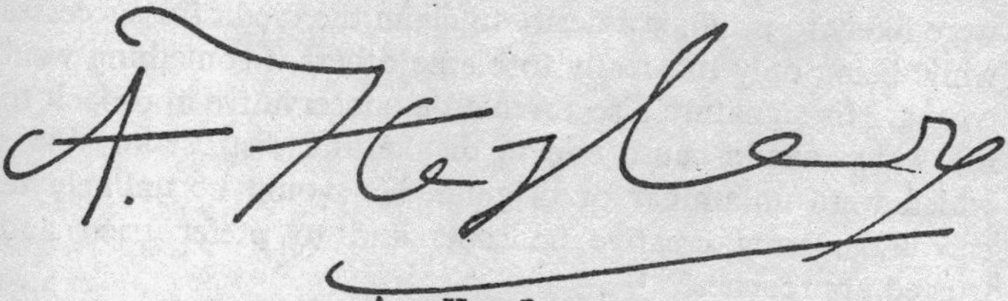

A. Heylery

(Creative Director)

Fig. 1.

One thing which A. Heylery's signature said loud and clear was that his attitudes towards life was bound to bring them into constant, and probably bitter, conflict. Here is the evidence provided by graphonomy on which we based our judgement. Sally's handwriting showed that she was liberal-minded, easy going, slightly emotional and extremely creative. She was an innovator with an extremely quick and flexible mind which was constantly seething with bright, fresh ideas. Because she produced so many ideas there was sometimes a danger of her being distracted from one task before it was completed. Sally also showed a strong desire for recognition and praise for her achievements.

These personality needs were fully met in her present job. Her immediate superior was sympathetic, perceptive and had a great admiration for her abilities. He too had a sharp, creative mind and the ability to see possibilities in a new idea. He also possessed the self-confidence to back something which was boldly original and to give ideas time to develop without putting on the pressure. When Sally was diverted from the task in hand he was able to guide her back to it tactfully but firmly.

We felt that she had found a creative, empathic working environment which gave the best support and encouragement to her talents. Would she find an equally agreeable atmosphere working with A. Heylery? His signature said that she was unlikely to do so. It revealed a strong need for status and a keen sense of self-importance. These aspects of his character were likely to produce a desire to claim the credit for successes while being only too ready to blame others if something went wrong. His signature also revealed a conservative approach to life which would cause him to dislike and distrust any ideas which were unfamiliar or original. He would be unlikely to encourage truly creative concepts and to prefer tried and trusted approaches.

Clearly Sally and her prospective superior had very different needs and abilities. We felt it unlikely they could work happily together and suggested she remain in her current job. Although she took our advice seriously, Sally found herself under considerable pressure from her husband to take the better paid, higher status position. With some considerable misgivings she did so, only to find her fears and our predictions fully justified. After a series of bitter arguments, which nearly caused a nervous breakdown, Sally left the job within a year.

Before we explain how it was possible to obtain such information from the signature, let us describe a second case in which it proved possible to reach an equally accurate conclusion about a person's personality and motivational needs from a signature alone.

Case History Two – The Right Man for the Job

Not long ago the personnel director of a major trading company approached us for advice about hiring a new sales executive. The long list of applicants had been reduced to just two names, but he was finding it hard to choose between them. Both had given excellent interviews and passed the other selection tests with ease. Their qualifications and experience were equally impressive and the interview board had been unable to come down conclusively on either choice. How could they be certain of picking the right man for the job? Was there anything in the handwriting which would provide a clue as to which of the two was most likely to excel in the working atmosphere of that company?

Based on the signatures alone we suggested that Adam Leonard would prove a better choice than Charles Maynard. As events turned out it seemed to be a sound judgement. But what prompted our choice? What was it in the signatures of the two men that strongly favoured Adam Leonard? Study the two signatures below and see if you can decide.

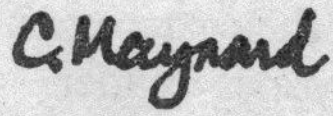

C. Maynard

Fig. 2.

Adam Leonard

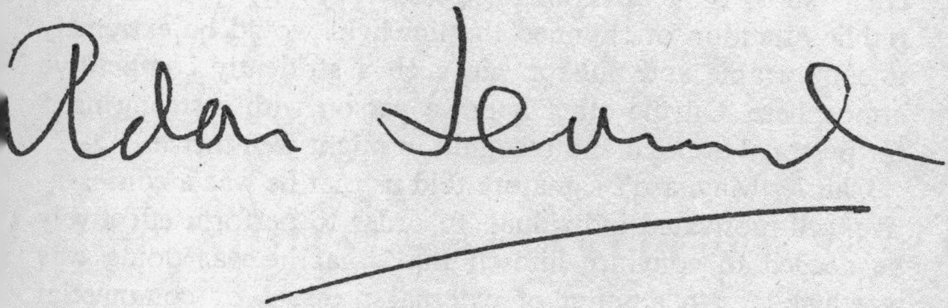

Fig. 3.

The first thing we considered was the way that particular company worked. Having acted as consultants to them on a number of occasions, talked to their staff and visited their headquarters, we had a pretty sound knowledge of their management methods. Perhaps because they were an American organisation, they tended to motivate sales staff in a rather theatrical manner. Not only did they pay the usual bonuses for above-target sales figures, but a high level of competition between the various sales divisions, and between the salesmen themselves, was encouraged. There would be regular working breakfasts at which those sales executives who had done particularly well would stand up to be applauded by the others. Any executive whose figures were below target would also have to stand up, explain his problems and listen to criticisms about his approach. Each month the firm's magazine published a sales division 'Roll of Commercial Honour' with the names of the top salesmen and praise for their achievements. Those who had made it to the roll of honour were allowed to wear a special pin during that month and received other recognition. At the firm's annual convention sales executives from the most successful division would be special guests of honour and go onto the platform to acknowledge a standing ovation from the other employees. Each would receive a parchment listing their achievements and be expected to tell the assembled audience how they had achieved their successes.

To survive and prosper under such conditions clearly demanded a person with a special kind of personality and particular sorts of motivational needs. Anybody who disliked public attention or shunned the limelight would be extremely uncomfortable and unhappy in such a stridently competitive atmosphere. On the other hand, a person with a strong need for personal acclaim and recognition might well thrive.

Charles Maynard's signature told us that he was a conservative, self-motivated individual. In order to perform effectively he needed to convince himself that what he was doing was worthwhile. No amount of external pressure or commercial ballyhoo would impress him. He also emerged as a rather retiring person who disliked being the focus of mass attention and took public criticism very badly.

Adam Leonard's signature told a completely different story. Here was a man who had a strong liking for external motivation. He judged his successes and failures by what others said about them, rather than any inner feelings he might have about his achievements. He had a powerful need to win public praise and would strive enthusiastically for such rewards. He was appointed and proved an excellent choice. Within two years of joining the company he rose to lead a top sales team, relishing the lavish praise of his employers.

HOW TO SEE INSIDE A SIGNATURE

Signature interpretation involves a consideration of four factors: Size; Style; Legibility and Embellishment. Of these the most important and revealing are size and style. You should start by looking at the dimensions of the signature and then go on to examine the way it has been written. Finally you study the only slightly less significant factors of formation and under-lining.

The Meaning of Signature Size

One of the most obvious differences between signatures lies in their size. Some are small and cramped, taking up only a tiny amount of the paper available to them. Others are bold and sprawl dramatically across the page. The signature size a person adopts tells us a lot about the way they see themselves and assess their own importance in the world.

The relationship between self-perception and signature size has been the subject of several major studies during the past ten years. Some of the most thorough have been conducted by Dr. Richard Zweigenhaft at the University of California. His research clearly shows that self-esteem is a prime factor in deciding how large, or how small, will be the signature. In one experiment Dr. Zweigenhaft gave subjects a bogus intelligence test, then randomly selected two groups from amongst his volunteers. One group was told they had done extremely well in the test, their scores placing them in the top 10% of the population. The second group were informed their results had been very poor. So bad, in fact, that they were in the bottom 10% of the population. There was, of course, absolutely no truth in these statements. The test was a fake which actually gave no measurements at all. The only thing which changed as a result of his announcements, therefore, was the self-perception of his subjects. As you may have guessed these differences were clearly reflected in their signatures. Those who had been told they excelled, significantly increased the size of their signatures, while those who believed they had done poorly, substantially decreased the size, by comparison with signatures obtained before the test was administered.

Self-perception is also affected even when the person is well aware that nothing has really altered but simply acts as if it had. This was shown in another of Dr. Zweigenhaft's intriguing experiments. He set up role-playing situations in which subjects were asked to imagine they were acting the part of important or insignificant individuals. For example, some might role-play the managing director of a multi-national corporation, or a political leader. Others would be cast as the most junior of clerical assistants or street sweepers. During the sessions the experimenters obtained signatures from all those taking part. It was found that subjects who were playing the high-status roles, or had been nominated as group leaders, increased their signature size.

In another study, carried out over several years, Dr. Zweigenhaft discovered that signature size takes on a permanent increase once a person attains a position of power and influence. A study of autographs by one of the authors (James Greene) has shown that the average height of the signatures produced by celebrities is 45% greater than that of non-celebrities. The two examples below make this point. Both were collected at a New York Ballet academy. The first is that of the tea-lady, the second belongs to Rudolf Nureyev who was in training there at that time.

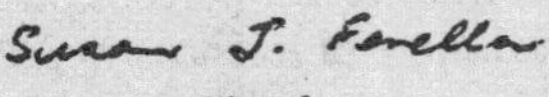

Susan J. Forella

Fig. 4.    Fig. 5.

The research results leave no doubt about the reliability of signature size as an index of the writer's self-esteem. It is also a reflection of temporary feelings of success or failure because the size is not directly related to the actual position of the writer but to the feelings of self-importance and confidence which usually accompany high levels of achievement. One would normally expect that an individual in a high status job to have a larger than average signature, but anticipate fluctuations depending on changing variations in success or failure. For instance a company director who has signed a multi-million pound contract may produce a larger than normal flourish of triumph on the dotted line. One who is signing a statement to the police after being charged with fraud may feel sufficiently subdued to produce a signature smaller than normal.

The triumph of victory and the misery of defeat are clearly seen in the two signatures of Napoleon below. The first was obtained when the General was at the height of his powers, the second soon after his surrender at Waterloo.

Fig. 6.
Napoleon's signature
before Waterloo

Fig. 7.
Napoleon's signature
after defeat

You can now see that signature size tells us two different things about the writer:

1. How much self-importance and self-esteem he, or she, possesses. This may be related to a high-status job or the belief that they are in an influential position. The reality of their situation is not important, only the *way* in which they see themselves is reflected in signature size.
2. Within these more or less permanent signature sizes, we also watch for temporary variations from one moment to the next. These provide a clear indication of the feelings of confidence or insecurity behind the writing.

In order to analyse signatures correctly, therefore, it is

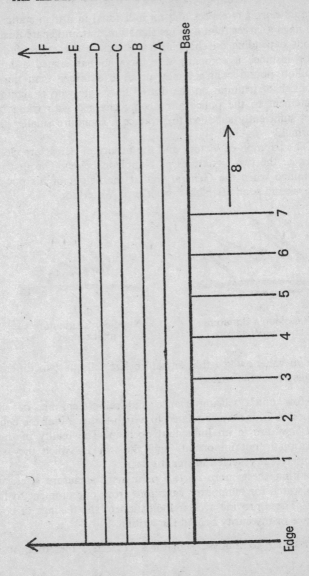

essential to be able to measure and compare them objectively. To do this it is necessary to construct a device called a Signature Grid.

CONSTRUCTING THE SIGNATURE GRID

You can either trace out the sample Signature Grid shown above on the Graph Tracing Paper (which we suggested you purchase in chapter two), or you can use a sheet of ordinary unlined tracing paper. The value of the Graph Tracing Paper is that the printed lines make it rather easier to copy the straight lines of the sample Grid more accurately.

Trace out the Grid with a ruler, using a pencil, biro or fibre pen. *Be certain* that you include all the lines, letters and numbers shown. Once the Grid has been drawn up it can be used over and over again on different signatures.

USING THE SIGNATURE GRID

Step One

Place the line marked *BASE* on the Grid under the signature as shown in illustration one (Fig. 8). If the signature slants up or down, angle the Grid accordingly. It is *essential* that the Base Line follows the bottom of the small letters in the signature.

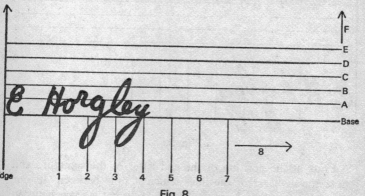

Fig. 8.

This does not mean the tails of letters such as 'g', 'j' or 'q' however. Follow the example given in the illustration and you should have no difficulty.

The first point to consider is how high up on the Grid the signature comes. Notice that, in the illustration, the letter 'l' finishes between the horizontal lines marked B and C. Where the paper limits of a letter comes between two lines, as frequently happens, *select the upper line* in order to assess the height of the signature. In our example the correct line to choose would, therefore, be Line C. Always measure the height at the tallest letter of the signature. Make a note of the letter which identifies the Grid Line.

Step Two

Now use the Grid to measure the length of the signature. To do this place the line marked *EDGE* against the left side of the first letter in the signature, as shown in Figure 9. The Base Line of the Grid must still be angled in such a way that it runs parallel with the base of the signature, as in the example.

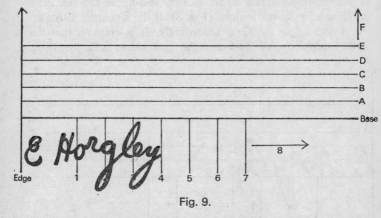

Fig. 9.

Look at the position of the end letter of the signature and note the *numbers* of the lines which it falls between. In our example the last stroke of the letter 'y' falls in the space between lines 3 and 4. Always use the higher of the two numbers, in this case 4.

You have now two references for that particular signature, a letter which indicates the height and a number which corresponds with the length. In our example the references for the signature of 'E. Horgley' are C and 4.

Now refer to Chart One which allows you to convert the reference points directly into a Signature Score.

Simply go *down* the chart until you find the appropriate letter (in our example this is C), and then *across* the bottom scale of the chart to the reference number (in this case 4). Where these two meet you will find the signature score. Against the references C4 we find a score of 2. This score can now be used to discover how the measured signature compares with the rest of the population, and to reach some important conclusions about the character of the writer.

Chart One - For converting reference points into signature scores

Grid Letters - Base Line

	1	2	3	4	5	6	7
F	1	1	1	1	1	1	1
E	3	2	1	1	1	1	1
D	3	2	2	1	1	1	1
C	4	3	2	2	1	1	1
B	4	4	3	3	2	2	1
A	5	5	4	4	3	3	3

Grid Numbers - Edge Line

Chart Two – Type of Signature

Signature Score	Type of Signature	Population Composition
1	Large	Larger than the signatures of 85% of population.
2	Moderately Large	Larger than the signatures of 77% of the population.
3	Average	Average.
4	Moderately Small	Smaller than the signatures of 77% of the population.
5	Small	Smaller than the signatures of 85% of the population.

WHAT THE SIGNATURE SCORE REVEALS

A score of 1 indicates that the writer will be a close match in personality and attitudes to those described under the heading *Larger than Average Signature* below.

A score of 2 suggests that the writer will be moderately close to the descriptions given in the larger than average signature section.

A score of 4 means that the writer will prove moderately like the descriptions given under the *Smaller than Average Signature* heading below.

A score of 5 means that the writer will be a close match in

personality and attitudes to those described under the Smaller than Average heading.

At this point you may like to go back to the start of the chapter and use the Signature Grid to assess the signatures of Rudolf Nureyev and the tea-lady. You should find that the dancer scores *one* while the woman scores *five*.

When discussing the significance of variations in handwriting pressure (chapter three) we stressed the importance of making a clear distinction between temporary and permanent changes. This caution is equally crucial when considering signature size. If possible, obtain a number of signatures produced by the same person over a period of time. Measure each of them and average the total to obtain a measure of the normal size. While doing so watch out for variations which reflect transitory feelings of self-esteem or insecurity.

Larger than Average Signature

People who always produce larger than average signatures have greater than usual feelings of self-importance and worth. They see themselves as in positions of power and responsibility, even when the status is only relative. For example, a big fish in a small pond is just as likely to have an above average signature size as a political leader whose decisions affect the lives of millions. As we mentioned earlier it is not the *actual* status which matters but the individual's perception of his or her own importance.

In either case they will have to be carefully handled if it is important to avoid conflict with them. Where the signature is considerably larger than average the writer is likely to have a somewhat fragile ego which can easily be damaged. He, or she, will probably be oversensitive to criticism, rejection and scepticism about their work, attitudes or ideas. Diplomacy and a certain amount of deference is necessary if you want to get your own way with such people. But the deference must never assume a patronising or abject tone, especially if the writing also shows indications of a high intelligence. They will easily see through such attempts which will then become counter-productive. Never try to oversell to this type of person, or attempt to force, coerce or overwhelm them. They feel important – and may well be important. Conversely, if you show any kind of weakness, subservience or inferiority then expect to be treated somewhat condescendingly.

These are not invariable responses, however. Where they feel their position to be secure, those with larger than average signatures may be willing to accept a certain amount of criticism without feeling under threat. They may also be too smart to behave in a condescending manner if this could prove disadvantageous. But, somewhere, their egos have a weak spot. If you need to relate well to such people be careful never to exploit that weakness.

Smaller than Average Signatures

This type of individual is the exact opposite of the big signer. He often does not have a very high opinion of himself and prefers to avoid the limelight. Such people may doubt their abilities and lack confidence. Although they may enjoy the benefits of a high status, if the role is forced on them, they are unlikely to actively seek acclaim and attention. They are more modest than the big signer and accept criticism more readily.

What should you watch out for in various relationships with people whose signatures are larger, or smaller, than average? As in previous chapters the most useful way of presenting this information is by considering it under the five different headings which, between them, cover all major forms of relationships.

WHAT SIGNATURE SIZES PREDICT

Big Signature Superior

May not take much notice of *your* needs for a positive self-image and importance in your job due to a possible exaggerated concern with personal status. Even worse, when things go well this type of superior may try to grab the glory and be unwilling to give credit to those who helped win the contract, design the product, reach the sales target or whatever else was involved in achieving success. If things go badly they may pass the buck to their subordinates. Such actions are carried out less in the hope of getting ahead than in an attempt to increase or defend feelings of self-worth and importance.

Small Signature Superior

Is not likely to take credit for the ideas and efforts of employees and is far more likely to pay attention to their needs and feelings. Will attempt to foster more of a team spirit among subordinates. However, if any of the subordinates are 'big signers' there may be a clash of personalities which could lead to strained working relationships.

Big Signature Employee

Could become a problem as he/she, attempts to enlarge their ego at the expense of colleagues. May be overbearing and attempt to steal the limelight. Will not accept criticism from superiors easily or with good grace. To handle this type of person you need to use considerable amount of diplomacy. Do not directly belittle his efforts. The best results will be achieved through recognition and praise for efforts and accomplishments.

Small Signature Employee

Can work well without constant attention and reward, because they are far more self-motivated. Unlikely to attempt to grab or hold the stage. If the signature is very small the individual is probably rather self-effacing and does not advertise abilities sufficiently. As a result, opportunities for promotion, although well deserved, may be missed. If you value the services of such an employee it will be essential to keep a careful eye on their work so that you can appreciate their achievements and skills. If you fail to watch out for such accomplishments they may never be brought to your attention and a worthwhile member of the staff could be insufficiently appreciated.

Big Signature Marriage Partner

Such a person will tend to put the relationship on a competitive basis, probably without even being aware of the fact. If both partners work then the one with the big signature will tend to resent any successes on the part of the other. This is most likely to be true if the man has a large signature and the woman enjoys greater rewards in her career. The most compatible situation is one in which a big signature person is married to somebody with a smaller than average signature. Where both are equally large there will be a clash of personality needs as each tries to assume the dominant role. This must inevitably lead to frequent rows, confrontations and disagreements.

Small Signature Marriage Partner

Where both partners have a small signature there will be little competition within the relationship. On the other hand, praise and flattery will be less successful as a means of influencing either partner's behaviour since they are little motivated by external influences. The most successful means of persuasion with this type of individual is to use subtle tactics which end up convincing them that some idea was really their own. This leads to a strong sense of self-motivation and the willing acceptance of the course of action.

Big Signature Friend

Do not beat this type of person too often at a competitive sport or game. They will not be good losers because they have a powerful need to succeed at all things. If they tell you some story or annecdote, try not to doubt it too openly – however far-fetched it sounds – as they take badly to criticism. Remember that the big signature person has an easily bruised ego and a constant need to have his, or her, self-esteem boosted.

If each of you has a big signature then be prepared for regular arguments and frequent disagreements as you both attempt to dominate the relationship.

Small Signature Friend

Less likely to try and dominate the friendship or to have a constant need to shine in any shared activity. The traits of self-effacement and a reluctance to take the limelight will be found in friendships as in most aspects of this type of person's lifestyle. Others will need to take the first step to get the friendship off the ground.

Big Signature Lover

Likely to believe that they are superb in bed and will be extremely hurt if informed too bluntly that they are not! If you want to improve any aspect of the relationship use gentle persuasion rather than sarcasm. May have an exaggerated notion of his/her sexual potency and attractiveness. Frequently people with big signatures have an intense need to prove themselves sexually. If such posturing is noticeable, regard the behaviour as an indication of a deeply felt fear of inadequacy – in bed and out of it. Competition between the sexes may produce hidden anger of which the individual is unaware. This can prove disastrous for any relationship, since such anger causes loss of sexual interest in the partner against whom it is directed.

Small Signature Lover

May lack confidence in sexual attractiveness and prowess in bed. Could be reluctant to take the initiative in developing a new relationship and may need to be led gently along. May require more than average reassurance that he/she is sexually competent. Will be less likely to dominate the relationship than somebody with a larger signature.

As you can see, signature size tells us a great deal about the type of person with whom we are dealing – and provides useful clues as to the best ways of handling them. But size is not the only key factor in signatures. You can also learn a great deal from the style which an individual adopts when signing their name.

THE SIGNIFICANCE OF STYLE

Your attitudes and feelings on a wide range of subjects are revealed by the style which you adopt when signing your name. Before we say anything more about this we would like you to carry out the name test below.

The Name Style Test

Below are four situations which would require a signature. Read the brief details and then sign your name as if you were in that situation. In order not to mark the book use a separate sheet of paper. The results will be just as valid – and as revealing.

Situation	Your signature
Writing a letter to the prime minister	
Signing your name to a notice to be circulated in the neighbourhood	
Signing a cheque	
Writing to a newspaper	

This test is derived from our own research and a study carried out by Dr Roger Boshier at the University of Auckland, New Zealand. He found that the ways in which we use our initials and first names reveals a great deal about social attitudes. First score your test and then we will explain what your score means.

How To Score The Name Style Test

Each of the name styles listed below is worth a certain number of points. If the way you signed your own name in each of the four situations corresponds in use of first names and initials to those below award yourself the points against each style.

Style Used	Example	Score
Names in full	John Smith	1
Initial and surname	J. Smith	3
Two initials and surname	J. G. Smith	3
First name, initial, surname	John G. Smith	3

Total the scores for each of the four situations. This will give you a maximum mark of 12 points and a minimum of 4.

Dr Boshier found that people who use the first style – with all names written in full – are more liberal-minded than those who adopt any of the other three styles. He came to this conclusion after a carefully controlled study in which a large number of subjects were first asked to sign their names as they do in the four situations which we described. He then

Social Attitudes Chart

Number of Points Scored	Attitude Rating
12	Conservative-minded
10	Somewhat conservative
8	Average
6	Somewhat liberal
4	Liberal-minded

administered a social attitude test and discovered the intriguing associations. Using this method we have conducted our own studies, in Europe and the United States, and obtained similar results. By referring to the chart below you can discover where the writer stands on social attitudes.

There will obviously be many occasions when you would like to find out something about an individual's social attitudes but cannot make use of the above test. However, it is still possible to obtain a reasonably good estimate of their ratings on the conservatism–liberal scale by looking at some examples of their ordinary signatures.

Style Used	Example	Social Attitudes
Names in full	John Smith	More liberal than average
Initial(s) and surname	J. G. Smith	Average
First name, initial and surname	John G. Smith	Average
Initial and Surname	J. Smith	More conservative than average

Dr Boshier concluded that the 'John Smith' signature style means that the writer is allowing more self-disclosure than when the 'J. G. Smith' or 'J. Smith' styles are used. Here the writer is 'hiding' psychologically behind the initials and will tend to be more formal and conservative than those who use their full names. Because of this, the signature alone has proved an accurate indication of that individual's position on a scale of attitudes which has conservative views at one end and liberal views at the other.

WHAT THE RATINGS REVEAL

If a person scored 10 or 12 points, then the comments included under the heading conservatism will, to some extent, describe their social attitudes. It is, of course, unlikely that all the remarks will apply in every instance. However, you should find that the majority fairly reflect that individual's attitudes towards major social issues.

When the score adds up to the average of 8 points, comments included under the headings of both conservatism and liberalism will prove appropriate.

Below 8, the score indicates more liberal social attitudes and you should find that the second section contains remarks which fairly reflect many of that person's views.

These descriptions of conservative and liberal attitudes are based on research carried out by Dr Glenn Wilson at the London University Institute of Psychiatry.

Conservatism

The socially conservative person can be generally described as an individual who is moderate, cautious and resistant to change. It is important to understand that the social attitude of *conservatism* has been shown by Dr Wilson's studies to be only minimally related to political conservatism. It is not, therefore, possible to tell how somebody will vote from their signature. Only the ways in which they see the world are revealed.

The socially conservative person has a preference for the conventional in all areas of life, from art to music and fashion to social institutions. The familiar is liked better than the novel and there is a marked resistance to progressive change, whether this is social or political.

The conservative individual favours militarism and feels uneasy about unconventional sub-cultures such as hippies and punks. He or she is patriotic, favours censorship and would prefer to curb certain sources of pleasure, especially sexual pleasures. There is a fear of dissent and anarchy. The conservative attitudes reveal themselves especially strongly in the area of law and order, where control through force rather than understanding is advocated. 'Do gooders' are deplored and regarded as one of the causes of the social problem rather than part of the solution. Religious views will tend to be orthodox and even fundamentalist.

The conservative attitude is substantially shaped by a distinctive way of looking at authority. Such individuals will defer to those in a position of power but insist on prompt obedience from their subordinates. Anybody with a signature style indicating a more liberal attitude is unlikely to be happy working for such an employer.

There is an above average fear for the future, combined with a fatalistic approach to life and a belief that an individual's destiny lies beyond their control. There is a dread of death and the unknown.

Social conservatism tends to run in families. As a child the extreme conservative often had a distant relationship with his/her father and was punished for any aggressive behaviour. This leads them to project their aggression onto other people. This is something which everybody does to a certain extent but it is more intense in the extreme conservative who tends not to have a very deep insight into personal feelings.

There is a dislike of 'sick' or 'sexy' jokes and a preference for puns, although the socially conservative person tends to find fewer jokes funny than the liberal whose taste runs more towards the 'sick' and the 'sexy' stories.

The socially conservative individual is a realist who shuns idealism and ivory tower theorising. He or she is tough-minded and looks for practical solutions to most problems.

Liberalism

Where the conservative avoids change, the liberal often seeks changes for their own sake. As with conservative attitudes such liberalism is only indirectly linked to a political attitude and does not indicate their likely voting behaviour.

People with such attitudes enjoy discovering new sources of stimulation, enjoy meeting people and seeing different aspects of life. They tend to reject establishment views and are seldom strong supporters of the *status quo*. They are candid, open-minded, and may be idealistic, although frequently lacking a practical approach to life's problems. A liking for the latest in music, the arts, fashions and ideas may make this kind of person overly susceptible to fads and trends at the expense of more lasting values. They reject censorship and feel that people should be free to express themselves as they please. They feel sympathy for the plight of minority groups and cultures and do not fear their influence. Rather they feel this will add variety and interest to society.

The individual with liberal social attitudes probably had a less punishing upbringing than average and was not expected to conform rigidly to parental attitudes and beliefs. Because of this, aggressive feelings may be openly expressed and such individuals are more prone to depression than those with conservative attitudes.

They are tender-minded and in sympathy with movements which aim at reducing suffering in the world, especially those which are seen as helping unpopular minority groups. The socially conservative individual, while no less willing to help cases which are considered to be 'deserving', is far more likely to support orthodox charities which promise less immediate relief but offer long-term benefits, such as research into heart disease, or cancer.

Signature size and style will, therefore, provide you with much basic and important information about the writer. But this is not the end of the story. We have not yet finished exploring the secret meaning of signatures. Those few letters still may contain a good many more details about the writer which it will pay you to investigate.

WHAT THE SCRAWLER IS TRYING TO TELL YOU

Some people virtually print out their names, others produce signatures which can be read with a little difficulty. There is one group of signers, however, whose names do not seem to have been written using conventional letters of the alphabet at all!

Some resemble examples of an ancient hieroglyphic while others look more like the death throws of an ink sodden spider!

Our research has shown that a major reason why some people sign their names illegibly is in order to convey a sense of their own superiority. By using a scrawl rather than a readable signature the writer is saying, in effect, that there is no need to clearly announce his, or her, name. Their status and importance are such that the reader of the document should at once *know* who they are!

A second impression that the scrawler tries to convey is one of working at high speed under great pressure. The implied message here is – 'This is all of my valuable time I can waste on you.'

It might be argued that there are times when busy people, company executives for example, *do* have to sign a great many letters and documents at high speed and under pressure. Under these conditions, surely, there will be a decline into illegibility. Our research shows that this is not, in fact, what often happens. Forming a signature is such an automatic activity that it tends to maintain its major characteristics no matter how fast we sign or how many times we have to reproduce the words.

Illegibility in the handwriting itself, rather than in the signature alone, tells us a different story however. It explains why people in certain professions, such as medicine, the law and banking, often write in such an indecipherable manner. Just what it means and why will be explained in the next chapter.

Embellishments

The Meaning of Underlining

The final point to note about signatures are the embellishments which some writers add. While such pen strokes are not a part of the actual signature they can tell us quite a lot about the writer. This embellishment is a line under the name, which does not add to the clarity of the signature but simply serves to emphasise it in some way.

Our research shows that this indicates several interesting things about the writer's personality. It is, primarily, an expression of confidence. Such writers feel they have an above average ability to cope with the daily challenges of life. They are more likely than non-underliners to take chances in order to achieve success and will more readily accept the blame for mistakes when they are responsible. This is possible because their confidence is far harder to shake than that of non-underliners.

The underlining embellishment is also a mark of enthusiasm and exhuberance. This is even more strongly indicated where the signature and its line slant upward.

The pressure used in underlining the name is also important. If it is heavier than the rest of the signature then the qualities of confidence and enthusiasm are increased. The heavy pressure underline represents a burst of excess energy left over after the signature has been produced.

Where the signature is underlined in an exaggerated or bizzare manner, as in the example below, it indicates that the writer wants to draw attention to himself and probably feels unable to do so in any other way. Unable to make his presence felt in a more immediate and direct way, the writer uses the

Fig. 10.

embellishment as a form of compensation. However, such a signature, despite appearances to the contrary, indicates a conventional rather than a nonconformist individual. The writer wants to attract attention but desires to do so through recognition of conventionally approved achievements. The decoration shown in the illustration on the next page was produced by a fifteen-year-old girl.

Such embellishments are often found in handwriting during the middle teens, as an adolescent strives to find a separate and distinct identity and personality. Other handwriting signs which show a similar striving towards identity will be described in chapter nine where we look at what handwriting has to say about development.

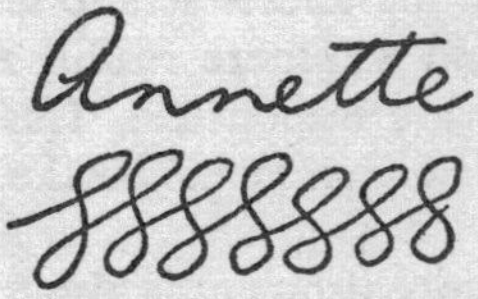

Fig. 11.

As you will now appreciate, signatures are a mine of information whose importance in carrying out an analysis is in no way related to the time they take to produce or the space they occupy on the paper.

With nothing more to go on than a signature it is possible to discover facts about a writer of which they themselves may be quite unaware.

In the next chapter we will be turning to an examination of the more specific aspects of handwriting. Applying the funnel method of analysis, which we described at the end of chapter two, we are now starting to focus our attention on the smaller aspects of letter and word formation. The correct interpretation of these characteristics allows us to make accurate predictions concerning what could be described as the very essence of another human being – their personality.

Chapter Six

Handwriting and Personality

Handwriting holds the key to one of life's most fascinating and tantalising mysteries – the true personality of another human being. Equally it can reveal truths about our own natures of which we were never previously aware. By means of the scientific procedures of graphonomy it is possible to penetrate the masks we so often wear in everyday life and discover the real person underneath.

All too frequently, trying to sum up somebody accurately is like sightseeing in a hall of mirrors. From moment to moment a different image appears. On one occasion an individual can seem friendly, on another reserved. We may notice expressions of aggression followed, perhaps, by signs of anxiety. Which of the varied impressions is correct? Which most honestly reflects that person's nature? Are they outward-going or detached, quick-tempered or controlled?

The same difficulty can arise when we attempt to analyse our own feelings. Some days we are relaxed and self-assured. At other times the world seems a hostile, alien place and we respond irritably and uncertainly to situations.

Everybody has moods and goes through moments of emotional crisis, and research has shown that a particular situation, and the behaviour of those around us, to some extent determines how we are likely to respond.

But, underlying these varying feelings, we each possess an inner self which is far more constant and resistant to change than transitory moods might suggest. It is this core of our psychological being, this unique *persona*, which determines our real personality. All too often, however, it remains concealed – even from ourselves.

We like to believe that we are good judges of others and of

our own natures. We imagine that assessments of personality are formed on the basis of careful observation and objective reasoning. Psychological research has shown that this is far from the truth. In one study it was found that people made up their minds about somebody else *within the first four minutes of their meeting*. Once that image of the personality has been formed, any behaviour which supports it is emphasised while anything which contradicts it is minimised. For example, suppose we conclude that a man is friendly but submissive. That judgement made, we pay special attention to all their responses which come into the category of friendly and submissive but ignore or overlook any unfriendly or dominant behaviour. If an incident which challenges our opinion has to be explained, we may say with a shrug: 'Oh, that's most unlike him. He's such a friendly, quiet person.'

So far as our own natures are concerned, we often form an impression of how people ought to behave and then try to act out the part. If we think that aggression is the only way to win in life, we may behave in an outwardly aggressive manner which runs contrary to our essentially passive personality. In doing so, of course, we create a great deal of unnecessary personal anxiety and unhappiness. It is only by recognising our true needs and feelings that we can live at peace with ourselves and the world.

Psychologists have tried to eliminate much of the subjective error in assessment by developing a number of personality tests. These range from various questionnaires through to famous *projective* techniques such as the 'ink blot test'. The intention is that the subject 'projects' his, or her, inner personality through finding images in an ambiguous blob of ink. The trouble with these forms of assessment is that they are sometimes very difficult to administer and even more difficult to interpret successfully.

Handwriting analysis offers an alternative which has neither fault. Not only is it easy to carry out an accurate analysis, and obviously no problem to administer, but such an interpretation can yield information about personality, your own or anybody else's, directly and unambiguously. It avoids the subjectivity of the projective test and the complexity of the questionnaires.

In a study by Dr. Kate Loewenthal, at London University, people were asked to assess themselves on such aspects of personality as 'originality' and being 'methodical' in their approach to life. Dr. Loewenthal then asked them to produce samples of handwriting which were given a group of judges to assess. Although these assessors had no knowledge of the writers at all, and based their judgements purely on the handwriting, they came up with a similar personality rating to that produced by the subjects themselves. Other studies have produced similar findings. It is perfectly possible to determine not only the character of individuals but often even their sex solely from a few lines of handwriting.

Why should writing tell us so much? Dr. Loewenthal's conclusion was that our handwriting is a form of self-presentation. Just like anything else we do for public scrutiny, for example the way we dress, our hair length, the wearing of jewellery and so on, handwriting represents a form of non-verbal communication. The difference is that while we can easily change our style of clothes, cut or grow our hair and present ourselves in totally different guise with very little effort, it is impossible to really change most aspects of our handwriting.

In chapter two we described the funnel method of analysis, in which one starts by considering the broad details, such as pressure and handwriting stress, then begins to focus attention on the finer details of letter and word construction. It is rather like an archaeological dig. The starting point is a careful, overall view of the site. When all the information which this overview can produce has been obtained, one can begin to dig downwards in a search for those small, but essential items which will reveal the intimate details of everyday life. In exploring the meaning of 'crystallised gesture' we shall be doing much the same – working down through layer after layer of the handwriting signs in order to discover everything possible about the writer concerned.

Our preliminary interpretation has now been completed. The

overview of the script has been made. Much of the information so far obtained has some bearing on the assessment of personality. Such aspects of an individual's behaviour as intelligence and activity level have a strong influence on the way personality traits are expressed. In chapter ten we will describe how all the information which can be obtained from an analysis, including details of emotional states and health, which will be described in later chapters, may be brought together in order to produce a full portrait of the subject.

In this chapter we will be explaining how handwriting can be used to determine eight key aspects of personality. Each section includes a scoring system which allows you to make an objective assessment of that particular trait. At the end of the chapter we will describe how you can use these scores to build up a Personality Profile of the writer.

The traits which we shall be exploring are:

Independence.
Assertiveness.
Submissiveness.
Perfectionism.
Ambition.
Extraversion.
Sophistication.

TRAIT ONE: INDEPENDENCE

In chapter one we gave a brief description of writers who leave out their 'i' dots. Because it provides such significant insights into the trait of *Independence* we shall be considering the meaning of the missing 'i' dot in greater detail here.

Writers who leave out their 'i' dots are likely to be more cheerful, resilient and placid than those who use them. They will be less concerned about the opinions of others, less fearful of the future and more active in their approach to life. Because they seldom brood on past mistakes they have a tendency to feel less guilt for their actions and may behave, on occasions, in an expedient or even ruthless manner. Their resilience allows them to go through a crisis without experiencing as much stress or fatigue as the average person.

They are self-sufficient, resourceful individuals who prefer to make their own decisions and then resolutely stick to them. They are unlikely to be great joiners of groups or movements and even less likely to be followers of others. In fact, such people are usually critical of social or group standards and may be rather lonely as a result.

As children they tended to remain somewhat aloof. Possibly they were early developers who preferred to make friendships among older children rather than peers. The missing 'i' dot therefore reveals certain characteristics of personality which are likely to lead to academic success. It is the sort of personality found among scientists and writers, but also among criminals. People with these traits are generally nonconformist, have a need for free sexual expression and many marry late. They like to extract themselves from difficult situations without help from others and to be alone at times of emotional stress.

They may find it hard to relate closely to another person, but when absorbed in a creative task they tend not to miss friendships. You often find that talking to this type of person is a one-sided affair. Their minds soar above the content of your discussion while they daydream about the latest project to have captured their imagination.

The greater the number of missing 'i' dots, the stronger and more consistent the above personality traits and the more independent the writer will prove in all areas of his, or her, life.

The missing 'i' dot factor is best assessed from a longish sample of handwriting which contains many 'i's. However, a short sample which contains only a few 'i's will be sufficient to give you a reasonable approximation of the writer's score on the trait of Independence. To obtain the score, look through a section of the script and roughly total the number of 'i's and note those which are undotted. There is no need to make a careful count, an approximation is quite satisfactory. The chart below will allow you to convert the proportion of missing 'i' dots into an Independence Score.

The 'i' Dot Score Chart

Proportion of 'i' dots missing	Score
All missing	10
Three-quarters missing	8
Half missing	5
A quarter missing	3
Only one or two missing	0

The higher the score the more likely it is that the statements made in this section apply. With a score of between 8–10 almost everything we have said above should be true about the writer. If half are undotted the majority of the statements will accurately describe that person's behaviour in most situations. If only a quarter of the 'i' dots are missing, many of the statements will prove correct in most situations. However, if only one or two of the 'i' dots have been missed out it is probably nothing more than an oversight on the part of the writer and little importance can be attached to it.

In order to start building up the Personality Profile make a note of the score for this trait.

TRAIT TWO: ASSERTIVENESS

TRAIT THREE: SUBMISSIVENESS

These traits are linked because they can be looked on as the opposite ends of a single personality dimension. Clearly somebody cannot be both submissive and assertive at the same time. While our behaviour is to a great extent determined by the sort of situations in which we find ourselves, there is a general consistency of response. Furthermore the same kind of handwriting sign can reveal either characteristic.

In order to assess this trait you must examine the sample of handwriting in order to compare the size of capital letters in relation to what are called 'ascenders', that is the letters l,k,b,f,h,d,t, where the letter stroke rises above the writing line.

Study the examples below which illustrate three different kinds of relationships between capitals and ascenders.

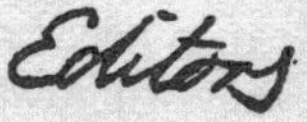

Fig. 1.   Example One

The capital and ascenders are approximately the same size. This is the most frequent style you will encounter and represents the average.

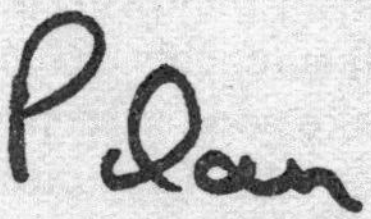

Fig. 2.   Example Two

Here the capital letter is higher than the ascender, a characteristic which is found in the handwriting of approximately 30% of the population.

Fig. 3.   Example Three

The capital is smaller than the ascender, a writing style found in approximately 20% of the population.

Research by Dr. O. L. Harvey of Boston has shown that handwriting in which the capital letters are *larger* than the ascenders (Example Two) is produced by assertive individuals. Writing in which the capitals are *smaller* than the ascenders (Example Three) indicates a submissive personality.

Dr. Harvey's study also established a close link between the difference in size between capitals and ascenders and the strength of these traits in the writer's personality. The greater the difference the more extreme the assertiveness or submissiveness of the person concerned.

The Assertive Writer

They are confident and dominant in relationships, can strike up a conversation with strangers easily and are not put off if the initial response is discouraging. They can ask for favours without feeling any embarrassment and have a strong desire to behave according to their own needs rather than those of their companions. As a result they will always try to put themselves in the most advantageous position, often even when this inconveniences those around them. This type of person speaks out forthrightly, defends himself vigorously when under attack and can talk frankly about personal matters without feeling self-conscious. In a quarrel they will have no hesitation about arguing openly and will staunchly defend their rights, even on trivial matters. They make good sales personnel but are equally effective in resisting sales talk. They rarely feel self-conscious in the presence of their superiors and welcome their attention when engaged in a task which they can do well. They seldom hesitate about complaining over shoddy goods or poor service. They make good hosts or hostesses and liven up a party. If they feel the need to flout social convention they seldom hesitate to do so, openly.

They make strong leaders, although in a position of power they tend to be intolerant of opinions which clash with their own views. If prevented from expressing these views, or if they feel they are not being taken seriously enough, the assertive individual can become quite irritated.

If this characteristic is found in writing which also lacks 'i' dots and has heavy pressure throughout the script, the writer will have a dominant and independent personality which makes him, or her, difficult to handle. It will take an equally dominant employer, a strong friend, a subservient employee or a devoted lover to survive the relationship.

The Submissive Writer

Such individuals are timid, cautious and passive. They find it hard to develop relationships and may not make many attempts to do so. Rather than push their own needs and wishes they usually yield to the desires of others. They hesitate to put themselves at an advantage if this means attracting attention. They find it difficult to resist persuasion from others and are uncomfortable in situations where they have to bargain.

They feel self-conscious when trying to talk about things which really matter to them and are disturbed by argument. If this kind of individual feels an injustice has been done then they are unlikely to make a scene openly, as they try hard to avoid rows. Then, anger will be concealed and may smoulder for a considerable time. They usually feel uncomfortable in the presence of superiors or when in the company of anybody with more knowledge or power than they possess. When the recipients of poor service or faulty goods their protests will be, at the most, mild. They hesitate before making introductions at parties, are uncomfortable in the role of host, and are unlikely to liven up a party. They seldom flout convention if this would mean drawing attention to themselves. Easily dominated they will go along with the wishes of a more assertive person rather than risk arguments. They dislike being made to take decisions and prefer to follow rather than to lead.

Scoring These Traits

The Comparison Chart below enables you to match samples of handwriting against the examples provided and so obtain an assertiveness–submissiveness score. Remember that it is important for size differences to be the dominant trend in the handwriting. A few capitals which are under- or over-sized should not be regarded as significant if the remainder are of equal proportions.

The higher the score on either trait the more strongly that characteristic will feature in the writer's personality.

You should make a note of the score obtained for this handwriting sign in order to complete the Personality Profile at the end of this chapter.

Comparison Chart

Example	Description	Score	
Blue Fig. 4.	Extremely High	10	A S S E R T I V E
Blue Fig. 5.	High	5	
Blue Fig. 6.	Ascenders and capital equal	0	S U B M I S S I V E
Blue Fig. 7.	Low	5	
Blue Fig. 8.	Extremely Low	10	

TRAIT FOUR: PERFECTIONISM

The handwriting signs described in this section are found in the script of people who are excessively methodical and almost obsessionally perfectionist in their approach to life. This trait has been carefully investigated by Dr. Elton McNeil and Dr. Gerald Blum at the University of Michigan. Their studies showed that three features of the handwriting were consistently associated with a perfectionist outlook:

(1) Small size of writing.
(2) Falling writing line.
(3) Crowded words.

Each of these is illustrated in the table below. In order to obtain a score on this trait you should compare the sample of handwriting under analysis with the examples provided. You will need to consider a sample of handwriting at least four inches in length to obtain an accurate assessment.

Perfectionism Table

Scoring Instructions	Comparison Sample
If the handwriting is as small, or smaller, than that opposite it scores 3 points. Fig. 9.	*Today in this our family,*
If handwriting is *larger* than the example above but *smaller* than that opposite it scores 1 point. Fig. 10.	*as soon as possible.*
If lines fall as much as, or more than the example opposite it scores 2 points. Fig. 11.	*we having small pox, subj begone I go out to*
If lines fall *less* than the example above but *more* than the example opposite it scores 1 point. Fig. 12.	*or Javanese with their emanated either from the*

Perfectionism Chart—*continued*

Scoring Instructions	Comparison Sample
If the words are as crowded as, or more crowded than, the example opposite it scores 3 points.	*The grapes are very*
Fig. 13.	
If the words are *less* crowded than in the example above but *more* crowded than those opposite it scores 1 point.	*Fresh fish is plentiful,*
Fig. 14.	
If the script is clearly rigid, as in example opposite add an additional 2 points.	*have passed change in*
Fig. 15.	

The final total will be between 0 and 10 points. This score can be used to help construct the Personality Profile at the end of this chapter.

As with the other traits described so far, the higher the score the more likely it is that the responses below will apply consistently to the writer.

The Perfectionist Writer

Like their handwriting they tend to be orderly and methodical, sometimes to an obsessional extent. They are likely to be overly neat, excessively concerned with small details and fussy about trivial matters.

This space-saving style of writing reflects a desire to conserve which is found in all areas of their life. They will cling to money, possessions and relationships. Because time too must be conserved they are punctual and hate being kept waiting. This causes them to be seen as reliable and conscientious.

They may strive for an appearance of moral superiority by condemning the activities and pleasures of others. The perfectionist writer is likely to 'go by the book' on every occasion, rigidly following the letter of the law and abiding by the pronouncements of those in authority. They will insist that things are done in accordance with tradition and pay meticulous attention to even the trivial tasks.

Aggression is more likely to be passive than open and frequently takes the form of obstinacy, stubbornness or a furtive resistance. After an argument with a close companion, the perfectionist writer tends to try and play on the guilt of the other party. He or she will attempt to make them feel responsible and sorry for the row. Sometimes they will go to elaborate lengths to win their way back into favour by this approach.

The perfectionist writer is generally undecided about the best course of action and is full of self-doubts. They have difficulty in making their mind up on many issues and in sticking to the point during a discussion.

The perfectionist personality is fairly common and will be encountered in many situations. To handle such individuals most effectively, stick to the following guide lines. Do not attempt to argue with them or their perfectionist goals and strict adherence to the letter of the law. This will only cause such a person to vigorously defend their position, by producing all kinds of arguments in support of order, method and obedience. In putting forward these justifications the individual will further convince themselves of the soundness of their attitudes and so make it even less probable you can get your point across! Never use emotional arguments since they are unlikely to impress such a person, since he/she admires logic above all else. Use this as your weapon in the discussion. Point out, logically and without emotion, any possibly unpleasant or inconvenient consequences of their actions. Try to do this without compromising the feelings of righteousness which such a person needs as a defence against self-doubt and anxiety. It is a hard task to make this type of personality change either their methods or their minds on any issue and doing so will take all your powers of persuasion.

TRAIT FIVE: AMBITION

In their computer studies of handwriting, to which we referred in chapter one, Dr. Elmer Lemke and Dr. John Kirchner discovered a single handwriting characteristic which can be used to detect the important personality factor of ambition.

Usually termed a *need for achievement*, it is a trait which has received considerable attention from psychologists. This is hardly surprising since the difference between success and failure, at all levels of endeavour, can often be traced to varying degrees of need for achievement. The schoolchild who does far worse than his companions in exams and tests may lack motivation rather than intelligence. The employee who fails to achieve promotion may miss opportunities through having too low a need for achievement rather than too little ability. Clearly this trait tells us a great deal about the ways in which we may expect the writer to behave under different situations.

The handwriting sign which allows us to assess this trait is easily identified. It is the downward pointing cross-bar on the letter 't' illustrated in the second example below.

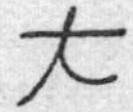

Fig. 16.
Standard 't' bar stroke

Fig. 17.
Downward 't' bar stroke

Since the majority of writers use a level cross-stroke, the slanting bar usually stands out clearly. The more frequently it is used the more ambitious the writer is likely to prove.

How to Score Ambition

Examine the handwriting sample and quickly count the number of times the letter 't' has been used. Now note which of the cross-strokes slants downward rather than moving horizontally across the page. As with the other signs we have discussed in this chapter, great frequency of use makes it more likely that the writer's personality will match the profile given below.

Ambition Chart

Number of Downward 't' bars	Score
All 't' bars point down	10
Three-quarters of 't' bars point down	8
Half the 't' bars point down	5
A quarter of the 't' bars point down	3
Only one 't' bar points down	0

You can use this score to build up the Personality Profile described at the end of this chapter. If the sign is found in conjunction with a larger than average signature and heavy pressure, discussed previously, it is even more likely that the personality characteristics described below will apply.

The Ambitious Writer

Need for achievement, as the term implies, refers to a strong desire to attain goals and objectives. Such writers will be very ambitious and have a powerful drive to prove successful at everything they attempt. Obstacles are regarded as challenges to be overcome as rapidly as possible. At work and at play they will exert all their effort to come out on top. It is not enough for them to stay up with the leaders, they want to be clearly seen as front-runners. Because they are so orientated towards success these individuals may be insensitive to the needs of others. They delight in competition which spurs them on to greater efforts, thrive on action and constantly seek to turn dreams into reality.

We are not, of course, saying that writing which contains the normal, horizontal 't' cross-stroke indicates a *lack* of ambition on the part of the writer. Highly successful men and women with a strong need for achievement may write their 't' strokes in the conventional way. What one can say, on the basis of the research studies, is that where the slanting stroke *is* present on the 't' bar that writer has high ambitions.

TRAIT SIX: AGGRESSION

Several recent studies have revealed that certain handwriting signs are associated with higher than normal levels of aggression. The main things to watch out for are as follows:

1: Pointed Dashes

Dr. Elmer Lemke and Dr. John Kirchner, whose researches we have already described in connection with other handwriting signs, have found that aggressive people tend to use pointed dashes of the type shown below. The more often these dashes occur the more aggressive the writer is likely to prove. They are the result of a sudden, impulsive stabbing movement as the writer finishes a stroke and can be found on any horizontal movement of the pen which does not connect one letter to another, for instance on the bars of the letters 'f' or 't'. Examples of these strokes can be found in the table below.

How to Score Pointed Dashes

Frequency Score	Examples
They are a consistent feature of the writing Score 3 points. They occur only now and then in the sample Score 1 point.	 Fig. 18.

2: Long Straight Upstrokes

These must not be confused with the anchor strokes which we described in the first chapter. The difference becomes quickly obvious with a small amount of practical experience. Anchor strokes curve down to meet the writing baseline. The aggression indicating upstrokes are straight and begin below the baseline. The difference should become readily apparent if you study the examples below.

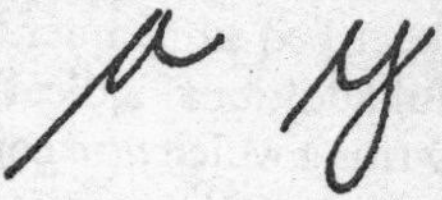

Fig. 19.
Aggressive long, straight upstrokes

Fig. 20.
Downward curving anchor strokes

How to Score long straight upstrokes

Frequency with which they occur	Score
Found at the start of three-quarters of all words or more.	3 points
Used on less than three-quarters of the words but still a consistent feature of the writing.	2 points
Found only once or twice in the sample.	1 point
If greater pressure has been used for these strokes than is present in the rest of the writing then add an additional point.	

3. End of Word Pressure

The examples below show end word pressure, with arrows indicating the actual pressure points.

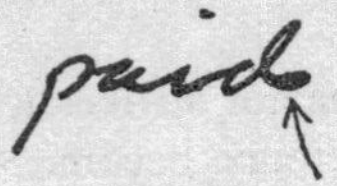

Fig. 21. 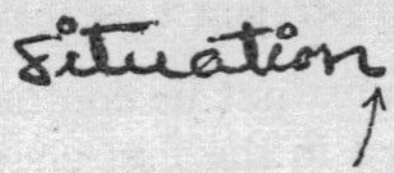   Fig. 22.

If this sign appears consistently in the handwriting sample then award a score of 2 points. If it is only present once or twice, in a reasonably lengthy sample, then award 1 point.

The final characteristic to watch out for is any sharp increase in pressure of the kind which was described in chapter three. This type of variation provides a useful additional indication of aggressive tendencies when found in writing which *also* contains any or all of the signs described above.

If several sharp increases in pressure can be found in the handwriting award an additional 1 point to the total score.

This will produce a possible maximum of 10 points on the aggression trait. The chart below allows you to interpret this score in terms of levels of aggression.

Aggression Chart

Personality of Writer	Score
Average aggression	0– 2
Moderately aggressive	3– 5
Aggressive	6– 8
Highly aggressive	9–10

A score of 3 or more indicates that the writer's behaviour will match the description given below. The higher the score the more strongly and consistently an individual is likely to respond in the way we outline.

The Aggressive Writer

Individuals can express their aggression either directly or indirectly. No matter which method is chosen, a high score indicates that aggression *will* be displayed on frequent occasions. When open, it can take the form of angry arguments, outbursts of temper, verbal cruelty, and perhaps even physical violence. It is rather difficult to predict exactly which form open aggression will take. However, if the writer scores high on the IQ signs in handwriting the chances are aggression will be expressed verbally, with sarcasm, caustic remarks, and mockery. A low level of IQ, which prevents words being used as effective weapons of aggression, makes it more likely that the individual will resort to physical force on occasions.

Where aggression is expressed indirectly the individual will feel a strong need for revenge if slighted. They will harbour a grudge and wait for an appropriate moment to get their own back. Exactly how this is achieved will depend, to a great extent, on the intelligence of the aggressive writer. A clever person may resort more to verbal attacks than physical assaults, relying on their intellectual skills to bombard victims with mockery, sarcasm and cruel jokes. The less articulate, unable to give vent to their aggressions using words alone, may resort to violence when their vocabulary of abuse runs out.

TRAIT SEVEN: EXTRAVERSION

An interesting experiment to establish the connection between the extravert personality and certain handwriting characteristics was carried out by Dr. Michael Williams of the University of Delaware. Dr. Williams and his associates gave people tests which, among other kinds of behaviour, assessed their levels of impulsivity and sociability. These are known to be two of the major components of the extraverted individual. Such people tend to act without thinking and to seek out the company of others.

Dr. Williams and his team then compared the test results with handwriting samples. A highly sophisticated statistical procedure, carried out on a computer, revealed three signs in the script which were consistently associated with an extraverted personality. These were:

(1) The slant of the letters.

(2) The width of small letters.

(3) The length of lower strokes, the so-called descenders. These include all letters which have a tail dropping below the writing line, for example g; j; and y.

The method for scoring your handwriting sample on the trait of extraversion is derived from our own and Dr. Williams' research.

Letter Slant Comparison Chart

Instructions	Examples
If the sample slants to the right as much as or more than the sample opposite score 3. Fig. 24.	*now is the time*
If the sample slants to the right less than the example shown above but as much or more than the sample opposite, give it a score of 2. Fig. 25.	*Having a super be in London*
If the sample slants to the right less than the example shown above but as much or more than the sample below, give it a score of 1. Fig. 26.	*too late for me night. so here's*

1: Letter Slant

An extraverted personality is indicated by rightward-slanting letters of the kind shown in Figure 23.

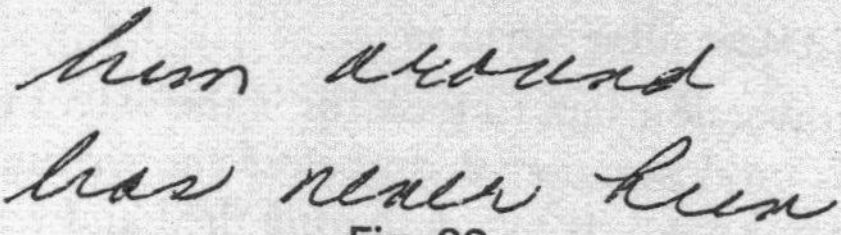

him around
has never him

Fig. 23.

The greater the rightwards slant the higher the level of extraversion.

You can score any sample of handwriting by making use of the Comparison Chart above. Simply match your example of script to those shown and note the score.

2: Small Letter Width

The wider small letters (i.e. a,o,e etc.) in the script the more extravert the writer who made them. You can score for letter breadth by comparing the handwriting being analysed with the chart below.

Letter Width Comparison Chart

Instructions	Example
If the small letters are as wide as, or wider than, the example below give it a score of 4. Fig. 27. *couple of days*	
If the small letters are narrower than those shown in fig. 27 but as wide or *wider* than those shown below give it a score of 2. *Pass by but they will never* Fig. 28.	

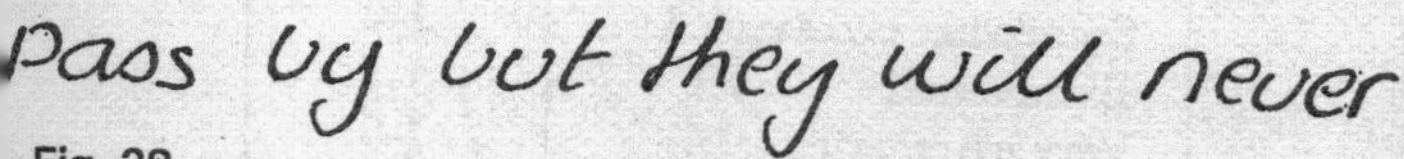

3: Length of Descending Strokes

The final extraversion sign to look for is the extent to which the lower strokes on descenders drop below the writing line. Once again make your analysis by comparing the handwriting sample with the chart.

Descending Strokes Comparison Chart

Instructions	Example
If the strokes are as long as, or longer than, those shown opposite give a score of 3. Fig. 29.	
If the strokes are not as long as those shown above but as long or longer than those shown opposite give a score of 1. Fig. 30.	

When making these comparisons there is no need to be precise. A careful study of the script, without the need for any rulers or other exact means of measuring letter size, is quite sufficient.

The total possible score on the trait of extraversion is 10 points. The table below enables you to interpret this score in terms of levels of extraversion.

Extraversion Score

Personality of Writer	Score
Average on extraversion	0–2
Somewhat extraverted	3–4
Extraverted	5–6
Very extraverted	7–9
Extremely extraverted	10

As with the other handwriting characteristics and personality traits, the higher the score the more closely the writer will fit the description of an extraverted individual given below. A score of 7 or more indicates that the writer will consistently behave in the ways we discuss.

A score of between 3 and 6 points suggests that the writer behaves in that way in many situations.

The Extraverted Writer

The factor that links an extraverted personality with a style of handwriting is the use of space. In everyday life extraverts have a physical and mental need for space around them. They hate to be confined. When writing, this space hunger reveals itself in a desire to cover as much paper as possible with their letters and words. The forward slant extra length, and overlong lower extensions represent a more extravagant use of paper than precise vertical lines, small lower loops and narrow writing.

Expansiveness, the keynote of an extravert's handwriting, is also the cornerstone of such an individual's social relationships. They are people who thrive in company and hate being left alone. Gregarious and lively they would far sooner spend the evening at a noisy party than sitting watching television or reading a book. When in company they tend to be like diners at an elaborate buffet. They constantly sample different groups, conversations and interactions, never remaining with any one for any length of time. Their friendships follow a similar pattern, they have quite a number but these are maintained at a fairly superficial level.

Professor Hans Eysenck, of London University's Institute of Psychiatry, who greatly developed the modern psychological concept of extraversion, observed that such people thrive on excitement and risk. They were prepared to take many more chances than the average person and never felt more alive than when living at high speed. They liked to laugh, take life lightly and play practical jokes on people. Because they are impulsive they live for the moment and do things without much thought, blurting out the first remark that comes into their heads, buying goods on impulse, often taking major decisions about their lives on the whim of a moment. They are easily bored and yearn for change and variety. They express their feelings more readily than others and often betray their moods because it is difficult for them to cover up inner feelings. They tend to be unreliable and may turn up late or fail to keep appointments altogether. Disorder and a lack of control in their lives does not worry them particularly. In fact, if anybody tried to introduce order they would quickly grow bored.

TRAIT EIGHT: SOPHISTICATION

Writers who produce the styles described here hope to convey an impression of sophistication by making their script distinctive and different. The two signs to look for here are the shape of 'i' dots and embellishments on the lower strokes of descenders.

Instead of the normal 'i' dot point the writer who is attempting to look suave and astute produces a small circle. They may also write the lower strokes of letters as shown in the illustration below.

| Fig. 31. | Fig. 32. |
| Circular 'i' dots | Lower Stroke Embellishments |

Occasionally one finds that writers who make use of these elaborations have developed a genuine sophistication but you should look carefully for other signs within the handwriting – such as a high level of intelligence – before coming to this conclusion.

Research has shown that the style is used by writers who are socially aware and somewhat emotionally detached. Their relationships may be exploited in order to help them achieve success. They often seem more like actors going over carefully rehearsed lines than people spontaneously expressing their attitudes towards others, tend to be somewhat sceptical in their approach to life and apparently have little faith in human nature. The dominant feature of this style is an attempt to appear shrewd, poised and sophisticated.

How To Score Sophistication

If the circle 'i' dot is present at all it is likely to appear consistently in the script. Score this 5 points.

Now consider embellishments to the lower strokes, which may occur to a varying extent.

If approximately half the lower loops have these embellishments, add 3 to the score.

If they are present in most of the lower loops, score 5. This gives a possible total on the sophistication scale of 10 points.

When analysis of this trait is completed you will have been able to rate the script on eight key aspects of personality. You should note that while some of the handwriting signs described in this chapter are excellent predictors of certain kinds of behaviour, their absence from a sample of writing cannot be taken to mean that the individual lacks these traits. One might, for example, find an aggressive person whose handwriting does not contain either pointed dashes or heavy pressure at the end of words. What one can say with confidence is that where these signs are present the writers will behave in the ways we have described.

By using the scores you can, if you wish, complete the writer's Personality Profile. This offers several advantages over merely noting the actual behaviours detailed in each section.

First of all it enables you to keep an easily interpreted record of each of the eight traits and to make comparisons between people with a minimum of difficulty. Secondly, you can compare different traits within each analysis and so obtain a clearer idea of how the writer will respond in different situations. It is important to realise that these traits, as well as other aspects of personality, such as intelligence and activity levels, are not distinct and independent factors but elements in a complex and dynamic interaction. The way they influence one another determines the overall behaviour of each individual. Only by considering the nature of these interactions, in the manner we describe in chapter ten, can a complete analysis be created.

The Personality Profile

	Score and Strength				
	None	Mild	Moderate	Sub-stantial	Extreme
Trait	0	1–3	4–5	6–8	9–10
Independence	0	0	0	0	0
Assertiveness	0	0	0	0	0
Submissiveness	0	0	0	0	0
Perfectionism	0	0	0	0	0
Ambition	0	0	0	0	0
Aggression	0	0	0	0	0
Extraversion	0	0	0	0	0
Worldliness	0	0	0	0	0

To avoid marking this book you may prefer to copy out the Profile onto a spare sheet of paper. Score by marking the box opposite the total achieved for each trait. Join the marked boxes, as shown in the example below, to produce an easily interpreted Profile.

The Profile below is taken from our cash history files. The writer was a 27-year-old man who holds the position of buying manager in a large London department store. Married with one young daughter, he worked his way up from the position of sales clerk and has been with the same firm for ten years. He is an attractive, outward-going person with many friends. In his job he needs to exert considerable authority and carries a large measure of responsibility.

On completion of his analysis we were able to produce a Personality Profile which looked as follows:

	Score and Strength				
	None	Mild	Moderate	Sub-stantial	Extreme
Trait	0–2	2–3	4–5	6–8	9–10
Independence	0	0	0	0	0
Assertiveness	0	0	0	0	0
Submissiveness	0	0	0	0	0
Perfectionism	0	0	0	0	0
Ambition	0	0	0	0	0
Aggression	0	0	0	0	0
Extraversion	0	0	0	0	0
Worldliness	0	0	0	0	0

This has been included here to demonstrate what a completed Personality Profile should look like. In the last chapter we will be drawing up similar Profiles for two other clients and showing you exactly how to assess the handwriting indications of each personality and how to use the Profiles to make direct comparison between two individuals.

Chapter Seven

Handwriting and Emotions

Emotions are among our most private and carefully guarded possessions. Some people hoard them like a miser's gold, spending sparingly at moments of extreme distress or intense delight. Others see them as shameful and indulge their innermost feelings only in private. A few seem willing to display emotions without inhibition, but one is never certain that their exaggerated joy or grief is any more real than the painted smile on a clown.

Small children usually show their feelings without restraint. Their laughter and tears are the most honest expressions and emotions we encounter – which may be why adults usually find them so touching. But, as children grow up, they learn to curb their feelings, to suppress and conceal outward signs of pleasure or pain. They discover that the free display of emotions often brings censure from adults and mockery from their companions. By early adulthood the training is usually complete. Honest feelings, especially those reflecting unhappiness or distress, have been locked up like dangerous beasts. With childhood behind us, we take pride in being 'self-controlled' and never letting others see when we are hurt or happy, fearful or frantic. There can be few relationships which would not be enhanced by greater insight into one another's true feelings. With such understandings how much better we might help those close to us. How much more readily we would sympathise in times of despair and share in moments of joy. How much greater our self-knowledge if we would only perceive and come to terms with our own carefully contained emotions.

The scientific analysis of handwriting offers the promise of attaining such insights. It is certainly not the full answer. But the procedures are a useful starting point on the road to deeper knowledge and more complete understanding.

In this chapter we are going to explore some of the ways in which recent psychological research has opened up this new approach to discovering a person's emotional state through an analysis of their handwriting. In order to do so we shall, as in previous chapters, be drawing on a wide range of research by numerous workers in Europe and America.

Handwriting contains clues to a writer's emotions because it is a self-recording gesture. More complex and more permanent than other gestures we make, but still the physical evidence of a complex series of bodily responses. Such movements are frequently the most sensitive indications of an individual's inner feelings. In a study of young children carried out by one of the authors (David Lewis), it was found that the under-fives can communicate fluently and silently using a system of non-verbal communication. Gestures and expressions, stance and direction of gaze allow them to convey a wide range of needs and feelings. Without saying a word, the child can request friendship, threaten aggression, express anxiety, solicit affection or offer co-operation. This language was described as 'secret'* because adults are so seldom aware of its existence.

As the child grows up silent language is gradually replaced by the spoken word. Although it is still present, and forms a crucial part of verbal communication, we usually fail to appreciate its full significance.

In order to suppress our emotions, we exert control over the more obvious aspects of body language. For example, we may smile, to cover up disappointment or anger. Or we may withhold the smile so as not to give the impression of being pleased. We often set the muscles of our face in a taut mask to prevent any clue to what is being thought and felt. We may avoid looking directly at the other person to prevent any indication of intimacy. Body language can be controlled, quite deliberately for a whole variety of purposes, but the control is seldom as complete as we like to think. An expert trained in the

* *The Secret Language of Your Child*, Souvenir Press.

interpretation of non-verbal communication can discover a great deal about a person's inner state through what have been termed 'leakages'. These are small, apparently unimportant, movements and gestures which may be the outward sign of an inner, but carefully suppressed, emotional turmoil.

In the face, leakage clues generally come from very tiny muscle movements and imperfectly executed simulations of an artificial mood. The smile which is drawn out slightly too long, the frown which is just a trace too severe. More frequently such deceptions are detected in finger, hand and foot movements: finger-nails digging into palms; fidgeting hands which pluck at clothing or carry out small acts of self-grooming – such as brushing down the hair at the back of the head. They include tense leg positions, restless or repetitive leg and foot acts, leg squeezing or soothing, aggressive footkicks.

All these and many other movements are carried out below the level of awareness. The individual concerned is not knowingly betraying his or her emotions, but the message is there for all who can see and understand it.

The same messages are hidden within handwriting and offer the additional advantage of being preserved there for as long as the written image remains visible. It is as if the writers had made a moving film of their body language and handed us a copy for examination. Best of all, emotions are easier to detect in handwriting than they would be on a filmed record. All you need is a little time, patience and the training provided in this chapter. Given these you should have no trouble in discovering the emotional state of any writer.

Our starting point, this time, is not the writing itself but the actual colour of the script. Where writers habitually choose to write in other than the conventional blue-black ink they immediately make an important statement about their emotions.

EMOTIONS AND INK COLOURS

When describing emotions we frequently use colour imagery; for example, people talk of 'seeing red' or 'feeling blue'; being 'white with rage' or 'green with envy'. We may describe some-body as in a 'black mood' or having a 'yellow streak'.

The ancients were well aware of the power of colours to influence moods. But it is only in the past few decades that an intensive study has been made into the effects of colour on the way we feel. To give an example, a vast amount of time and money has been invested in discovering the most soothing colours for airport lounges and aircraft interiors, so as to calm the nerves of anxious passengers. Psychologists have shown that people in rooms decorated a deep blue undergo a decrease in emotional response. Greens are associated with a calm, tranquil environment while browns are preferred by more introverted individuals.

Because of this close association between colours and emotions the writer's choice of ink, when made consistently and from preference, can reveal his, or her, inner feelings.

A study carried out by Psychiatrist Dr. William Rottersman, for the United States Marine Corps, showed that ink colour alone could provide a useful indicator of a recruit's suitability for military service. His research revealed that while there was a rejection rate, on psychological grounds, of only 10% of men who habitually wrote in blue-black or black ink, this rose to 50% among those using green ink by choice. This latter group also shared a number of distinctive emotional characteristics.

Fear of ridicule and appearing different made it impossible for them to express their individuality adequately. In addition most reported an over-dependence on their mothers, or some mother substitute such as a wife, mistress or teacher. Dr. Rottersman concluded that they were trying to 'make up' for this dependency by striking an apparently trivial blow for their individuality through the use of green ink. After extensive interviews, which went deeply into their family backgrounds and outward behaviour, he reached the opinion that, in many cases, their emotional problems were so serious as to make them unsuited to military life.

While our own research has not indicated that green ink writers would necessarily be unsuitable for military service, it has confirmed many of Dr. Rottersman's findings about the emotional characteristics of people who prefer to use such ink.

We have found that they do possess a hidden desire to be nonconformist and to assert their individuality. Because they are also afraid of looking foolish if such behaviour was expressed openly, however, these desires are restricted to the world of dreams and fantasy. They often live a Walter Mitty-like existence, picturing themselves being the focus of attention through carrying out some dramatic activity. Sometimes you can catch a hint of what is going on in their inner world through some minor strategy which is designed to demonstrate their individuality in a fairly unobtrusive manner. They may, for example, wear a lapel pin or badge which is unusual or original. If they drive a car, such writers may place a plastic model on the dashboard or in the rear window. They may also adopt an unusual phrase or saying, making it into a personal catch-phrase which serves to provide them with a more interesting identity. In this way they can be seen as attempting to get the best of both worlds, to stand out in the least obtrusive manner possible and to exert their personalities without taking any risks of ridicule or rejection.

In order to relate satisfactorily to this type of person it is important to take charge tactfully and guide them gently towards a desired goal. When the green ink writer is a man, he is likely to be more than usually passive and to find it difficult to take decisions. Such writers can be helped to express individuality by taking an interest in any creative activities they undertake. Be careful never to imply that their actions are in some way eccentric or unconventional since they are extremely sensitive on such points. Dr. Rottersman's study also included an investigation of the personalities of writers who preferred to use red ink. They were, he concluded, far more disturbed than green ink users and often exhibited bizarre symptoms quite openly. Many were either borderline or actual cases of mental illness.

We must stress that these descriptions will only hold true if the writer is known to use green or red ink *habitually* and as his or her *preferred choice*. They do not tell us anything about a person's emotional state if they just happened to pick up a pen which contained coloured ink because no other one was available at the time. Neither do they apply if green or red ink is simply used to make corrections to a text written in conventional ink colours.

Writers who habitually and from choice use *black ink* are not so much revealing an emotional state as an attitude towards communication. However, we mention this colour of writing ink here for the sake of completeness. Such individuals are concerned with precision, exactitude and in the clear under-standing of all aspects of the message they are attempting to convey. They have a strong desire to make themselves clear and to avoid confusions. Frequently the use of such ink is associated with people in professions which demand a high degree of precision, such as accountancy, engineering, mathematics and so on.

EMOTIONS AND WORD FORMATION

When a word has a special emotional importance for an individual, this is sometimes revealed by the way it is written. For example, compare the word 'happiness' in the sample below with the rest of the writing. It was written by a man who had experienced several unsatisfactory love affairs and whose overwhelming concern about the concept of happiness is clearly shown in the way he wrote the word.

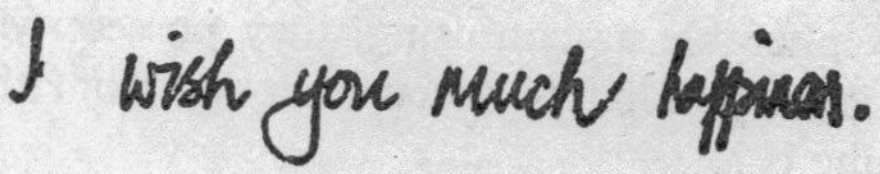

Fig. 1.

The sample below was written by a girl who worked in advertising but deplored the high pressure sales techniques she was told to use in order to secure new accounts. Her hand-writing shows her to be a sensitive individual who dislikes being aggressive and pushy. Note the word 'ruthless'. It is cramped and barely legible, an indication of her true feelings about the ruthless behaviour necessary in her work.

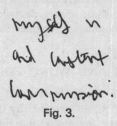

It was a ruthless way of

Fig. 2.

Aspects of the writer's emotional make-up are also revealed by several types of illegibility in the scripts. There are two major reasons why handwriting should be difficult to read, but only one of them is associated with emotions. The first type of failure of legibility is caused by lack of control over the writing muscles due to inadequate learning or poor co-ordination. An illustration of this type of illegibility is shown here:

myself in and constant compassion.

Fig. 3.

Unreadable writing which serves a writer's emotional needs has a special form of illegibility which makes it quite distinctive. In the first instance *none* of the words can easily be read. In the second only a few words are unclear and these can usually be understood in the context of the writing. Not so much indecipherable as confusing, they possess what we call *isolated ambiguity*. That is, when removed from the sentence their meaning is lost.

A good example of this *isolated ambiguity* is shown below. Unlike the sample above the words can be read easily when seen in context. But if the word 'going' is isolated from the remainder, by covering the others over, it becomes ambiguous. Now the meaning might be 'gairg', 'gang', or 'gamg'. The strokes have been formed well enough but the finished result is open to several interpretations. Perhaps without even being aware of the fact, this writer has developed a style which inhibits clear communication.

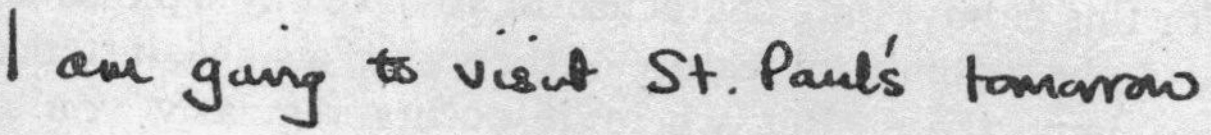

I am going to visit St. Paul's tomorrow

Fig. 4.

Isolated Ambiguity

Our research has shown that such writers dislike making their meanings clear. They prefer to offer an ambiguous message which is left up to the other person to interpret. They are overly concerned with concealment, with covering up and keeping aspects of their personalities or private lives not so much hidden from view as cloaked in mystery. We are not told a lie, rather we are offered their particular version of the truth. There may be several reasons why isolated ambiguity appears in the handwriting, none of which have anything to do with the personal integrity of the writer.

For example, we have found that isolated ambiguity is often present in handwriting of people whose professions demand a high degree of confidence-keeping, such as lawyers, bankers and doctors. This is especially true in the last occupation where not only must secrets be kept *about* the patients, but information often withheld *from* them. It also requires a large amount of tact, plus on occasions a certain ambiguity of response, to provide facts in the most reassuring manner possible. The same applies, to some extent, to lawyers, bankers, diplomats and politicians and often reveals itself not only in their words but in the ambiguous way in which some of these words are formed.

It is wrong to interpret isolated ambiguity as a sign of a deceitful personality. The important question is what the writer could be attempting to conceal and why. A letter from your doctor may contain isolated ambiguity as a result of training, not because he, or she, is untrustworthy. But the same amount of ambiguity in a personal letter from an intimate companion needs to be considered rather differently. It may reveal feeling of insecurity or inadequacy, or there may be some aspect of their personality or background which causes them such embarrassment they feel compelled to keep it hidden.

For this handwriting characteristic to have any significance it needs to be a dominant feature of the script; a single instance is of no importance. But where it occurs regularly you can interpret isolated ambiguity as a concealing tactic which reveals the writer's desire to hide something from the world.

HANDWRITING AND EMOTIONAL DISTURBANCE

There are occasions in everybody's life when emotions take control. When we worry excessively or experience deep feelings of guilt. When our sleep is disturbed and concentration impaired because of an emotional response too powerful for us to handle. Usually, after the crisis passes, we are able to cope with our feelings as effectively as before. Problems shrink to their right perspective, we no longer feel miserable or rejected, anxious or threatened. We again sleep at night and concentrate on our daily affairs without difficulty.

But for many people a high level of emotional disturbance is no temporary state of distress. It is a permanent response to everyday life. So common is this difficulty that Professor Hans Eysenck of the Institute of Psychiatry has estimated that it may be experienced by as many as one third of the population.

The runaway emotions of the disturbed person leave clear indications in the handwriting. Because different people express such disturbance in different ways, the signs within the script vary from one writer to the next. However, if three or more of the major characteristics of emotional disturbance are present in a sample of handwriting you can be reasonably certain that this is a dominant trend in that individual's life. As with other indications, the more frequently they occur and the wider the variety of signs, the more highly disturbed the writer is likely to prove. Before describing the various responses which you can expect to find in such a person's behaviour, here are the handwriting signs to watch for.

Back Slant

The leftward slope to the writing below represents an unnatural style which you will not find taught in any school. Nor is it particularly related to lefthandedness.

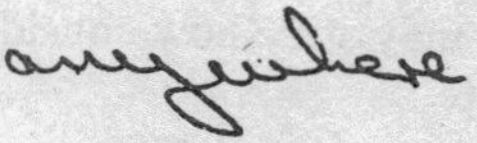

Fig. 5.

The construction of the human hand and the left to right flow of Western writing, means that the forward slant, whose connection with extraversion was discussed in the last chapter, is the easiest to produce. Less muscular effort is necessary because the slant moves forward with the writing impulse much like a swimmer being swept along by a powerful current. The backward slope, by comparison, requires considerable muscular effort because it represents a force exerted away from the forward progress of the script. This time the swimmer is fighting against the pull of the current. It is as if, by fighting against the natural writing flow and exerting needless effort in the attempt, the writer was symbolising both a perpetual struggle with the world as well as a desire to pull back and withdraw from the onward momentum of life.

In a study of the handwriting of many hundreds of emotionally disturbed people, we found a far greater tendency to adopt a backward slope than occurs in the rest of the population. For example, while the handwriting of emotionally balanced writers has only a 15% incidence of backward-sloped letters, we discovered that 58% of people with a phobic difficulty showed this type of slant. In the handwriting of men and women who had sought clinical help for an anxiety problem the backward slope occurred in 45% of cases.

Slant Variability

Some people manage to maintain an even slant, with all the letters tilted in more or less the same direction, as in Figure 6 below. The other writers seem unable to achieve this consistency, and the slant of their writing swings first one way and then another. Figure 8 shows an example of such slant variability. Notice that the letters sometimes slant right and other times left. Although the writing may have a dominant slant to either left or right it may still show considerable variability as the examples illustrate.

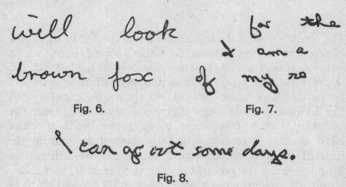

Fig. 6.   Fig. 7.

Fig. 8.

The samples of handwriting above can be used to estimate the amount of slant variability in a script.

If the slant variability is no more pronounced than in Figure 6 it may be considered perfectly normal.

If the slant varies as much as, or more than, the samples in Figure 7 and Figure 8 then emotional disturbance on the part of the writer is suggested.

Small Letter Variability

This indication of disturbance is illustrated in Figure 10. Notice that the small letters ('a', 'o', 'u', etc) show marked variations in sizes as compared with the writing of a non-disturbed individual.

Fig. 9.
Normal Variability

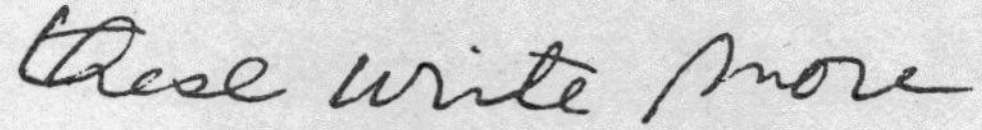

these write more

Fig. 10.
Variability Indicating Emotional Disturbance

As with slant variability you can use the examples to assess any piece of handwriting. If the small letter variability is as great as, or greater than, that shown in Figure 10 then it may be taken as strongly suggesting emotional disturbance.

The reason why such variations are associated with emotional problems is complex. In fairly simple terms however the irregularity occurs because of an uneven flow of commands from the brain to the writing muscles. Instead of a smooth stream of orders, there is an unbalanced emphasis first on one group of muscles and then on another. This leads to the variability of the letters while equally indicating an imbalance in the person's emotional functioning.

Narrow Upper Loops

An anxiety-produced restriction of the forward movement in handwriting results in the narrow upper letter loops illustrated below. The muscles which propel the pen towards the right side of the paper are tense and so impede the natural movement of the script.

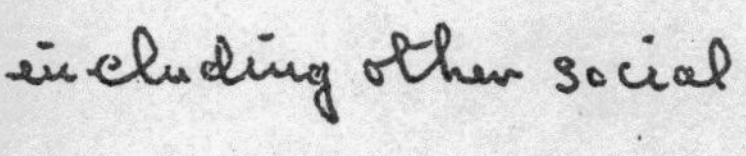

including other social   *which levels idirectly*

Fig. 11.   Fig. 12.
Normal Upper Loops   Narrow Upper Loops

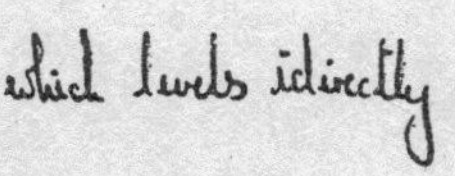

Line Overlap

Dr. O. L. Harvey of Boston discovered this association between a handwriting style and anxiety difficulties. It occurs when the strokes from one line impinge on the line below as shown in Figure 13.

Notice how the lower loops of the 'y' and 'g' touch the letters beneath them. Where the anxiety difficulty is pronounced this

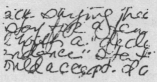

Fig. 13.

can produce an even more extreme form of overlap which is illustrated in Figure 13. Here the lines of writing have become entangled like skeins of knitting wool.

Waviness of the Writing Line

This is an extremely distinctive characteristic of the handwriting produced by emotionally disturbed individuals. Notice, in the example below, how the writing snakes along the page.

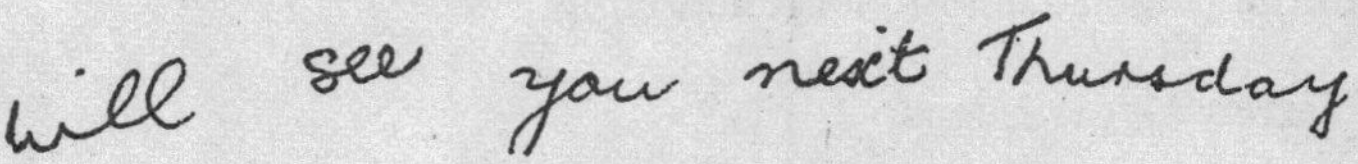

will see you next Thursday

Fig. 14.
Wavy line writing

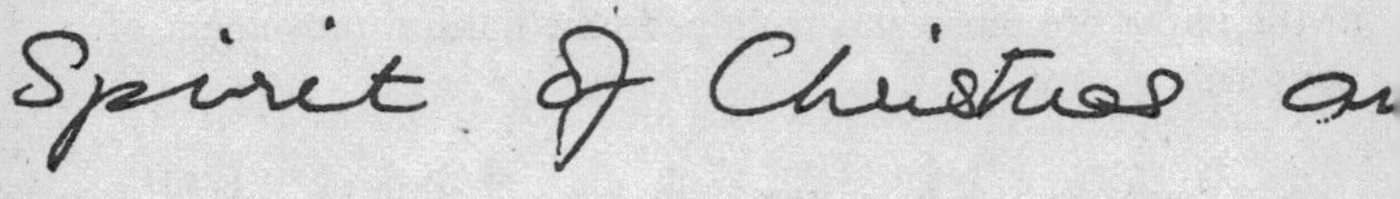

Spirit of Christmas a

Fig. 15.
Normal line writing

This unevenness becomes even more apparent when the normal and disturbed handwriting lines are compared. It is caused by momentary lapses in the writer's attention which upsets the visual feedback essential in order to produce a straight line of script. The breaks in concentration are brief rest pauses when, momentarily, the writer loses track of the line direction.

Poorly Co-ordinated Writing

Unless due to some physical problem such as brain damage, the poor co-ordination shown in Figure 17 can be taken as a sign of emotional disturbance.

With three or four

there will be people

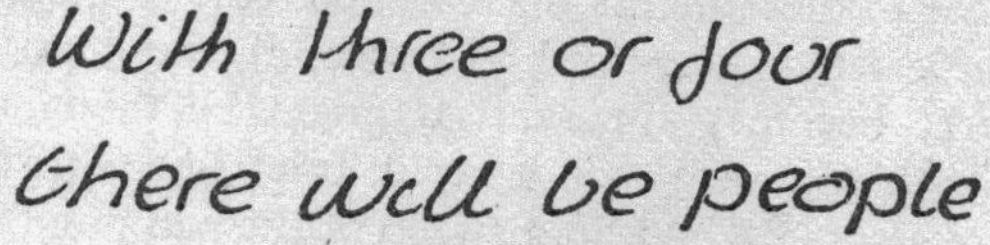

Fig. 16.
Normal Handwriting

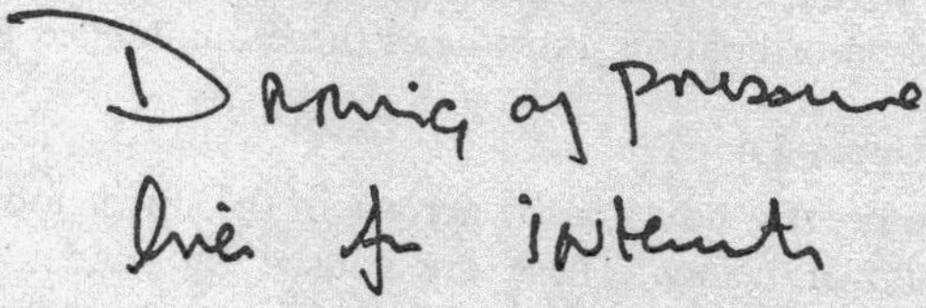

Fig. 17.
Poorly Co-ordinated Handwriting

A comparison between these two samples should make the effects of poorly co-ordinated writing easy to identify.

The last two handwriting characteristics we want to consider are slightly harder to detect than the signs already described. A magnifying glass ($\times$ 3 magnification is sufficient) will prove useful in identifying these symptoms of emotional disturbance, both of which are to be found within individual letters.

Stroke Jerks

The arrows against the handwriting sample below indicate where there have been small but sudden departures of the pen from its intended direction.

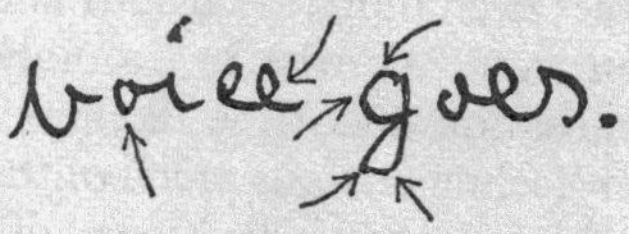

Fig. 18.

If you examine the letters carefully you will see that, instead of the smooth stroke which the writer clearly intended, there are slight bends in the line. When one considers how little time it took to create these marks on the paper (the average letter is formed in less than one-third of a second), the importance of stroke jerks becomes apparent. It might be thought almost impossible to complete such a rapid, brief line with anything other than a smooth and fluid sweep of the pen point. That is, indeed, the way in which most people form their letters. The anxious writer, however, because of additional tension and disturbed co-ordination, introduces these unintended jerks.

Broken Upper Loops

Note the breaks indicated by arrows in the upper loops in the words shown below. These are caused by sudden pressure losses as the muscles of the hand are released to move the pen point upwards. As with the other types of disorder described above, our research has shown that this is caused by excessive anxiety.

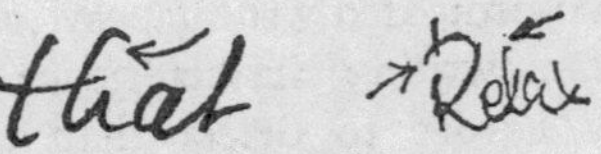

Fig. 19.

The Emotionally Disturbed Writer

If three or more of the handwriting signs we have described above are present in the sample then, as we said earlier, you should consider that the writer is emotionally disturbed. If there are five or more signs present you are most probably dealing with the script of a highly disturbed person. Needless to say, conveying details of your analysis to the subject, always a tricky task, becomes even more hazardous and delicate in such cases. In fact, you would be wise to do more than produce a comforting generalisation about the likelihood of their 'living on their nerves' or 'feeling anxious much of the time'.

However, by identifying indications of emotional disturbance early enough it is often possible to help the writer bring their troubles into a more realistic perspective. If these signs begin to appear in your own writing, take time out to consider what may be causing your emotional difficulties and how you can best resolve the more pressing of them. The sensitive nature of handwriting, as an external indicator of internal distress, often allows emotional disturbances to be discovered before they have become a powerful enough influence to have a serious effect on the writer's life.

What sort of behaviours and responses can one expect from the emotionally disturbed person? Studies by Professor Eysenck enable a clear portrait to be created of this type of individual.

He, or she, will be nervous, excitable and have a tendency to worry excessively, not just about everyday problems but even over extreme and unlikely events.

They experience greater guilt than other people, are more prone to depression and often appear deeply unhappy. Their sleep is interrupted, their concentration is often poor, and they may appear somewhat forgetful.

These emotional reactions often interfere with the person's judgements and responses to the demands of work, play and intimate relationships. They are likely to reach decisions irrationally and may behave in a way which makes failure a more probable outcome than success. Their responses to situations may also be extremely rigid. They often develop a particular way of doing things and continue with that style however inappropriate it becomes.

They become nervous or emotional in situations which would not worry emotionally balanced individuals.

The most usual response of an emotionally-disturbed individual is to try and avoid problems by adopting some tactic which prevents a confrontation with the real issues. This can be a mental avoidance, with the whole difficulty simply being ignored or repressed. But it may also take the form of physical avoidance with a refusal to attempt certain tasks or to enter situations which cause anxiety.

The underlying feature of all these responses is that of inner conflict. There is a clash between the individual's feelings about how they should, *ideally* behave and the reality of what that person feels capable of actually doing. The outward sign of this confusion may be an inconsistency of behaviour. For a time the person will attempt to regulate every aspect of their life, forcing emotions into a sort of mental strait-jacket that prevents any expression of feelings. Then, all at once, restraint may give rise to excess during which little or no effort seems to be expended in enforcing control over all aspects of their lifestyles.

Emotional Constipation

This vivid phrase is used by psychologists to describe people who have an emotional blockage which is just as uncomfortable and distressing as a physical one. In sharp contrast to the type of emotional disturbance described above, such people are quite unable to give free vent to their feelings. Their emotional control is total and consistent. In situations which would cause most people great joy or grief they remain impassive and uninvolved, the faces revealing no sign of feelings. Because they seem so utterly cold and, sometimes, inhuman, emotionally constipated people find it hard to maintain close relationships or to be very much liked by others. They make matters worse by feeling considerable embarrassment and discomfort in the presence of people who can readily display their emotions.

Because they feel incapable of expressing emotions, which they fear and distrust, such people tend to remain calm and cool in situations which might cause others to panic. This is sometimes to their advantage, but because they are unable to respond appropriately at times when deep feelings must be expressed they lack any empathy.

Individuals who exercise effort to curb their emotions will exert an equal amount of energy in curtailing other natural impulses in their handwriting. Whenever they feel that the writing movement is threatening to get away from them they immediately apply restraints. This creates distinctive features in the script which allow you easily to distinguish the emotionally constipated writer.

Handwriting and Emotional Constipation

The most common form of handwriting restraint is found in the curtailment of follow-through in word or letter endings. In the examples below arrows indicate the points where the writer has restrained the writing impulse when the forward momentum threatened to escape from their control.

The effect is to produce a series of clipped movements. Such 'chopping off' of the letter strokes demands a considerable amount of muscle effort, especially where the curtailment is very sharp as in the lower extensions (arrowed) of the first example.

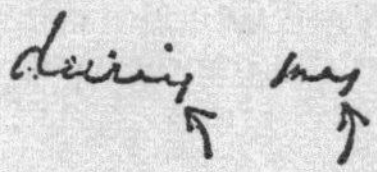

Fig. 20.

Further 'chopping off' of the impulse can be seen in the 'd' of 'caused' and 'forward' below. Notice also the curtailment of the end stroke in the word 'been'.

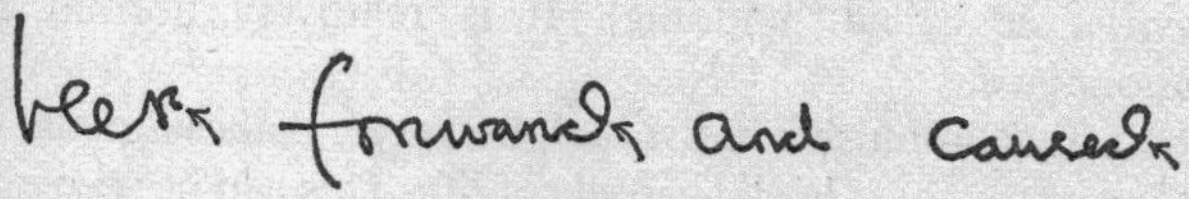

Fig. 21.

You will see that most of these curtailments have been executed with increased pressure, a fact which emphasises the impression that the writer has applied strong measures to control the forward movement. It is rather like a person free-wheeling down a hill on a bike, finding that the brakes have failed and digging his feet into the road in order to stop.

Such signs are a clear indication that the writer avoids spontaneity and carefully considers actions and statements before producing them.

Other commonly encountered types of curtailment are shown below. These are worth studying as you will be very likely to encounter them in the handwriting of emotionally blocked writers. But bear in mind that they represent only a few of the many examples which can occur. Because handwriting is such an individual means of expression, curtailments and other characteristics can be expressed in a wide variety of ways. It would be virtually impossible to list all of them and quite unnecessary. You need simply bear in mind that such 'chopping off' of strokes is associated with emotional constipation.

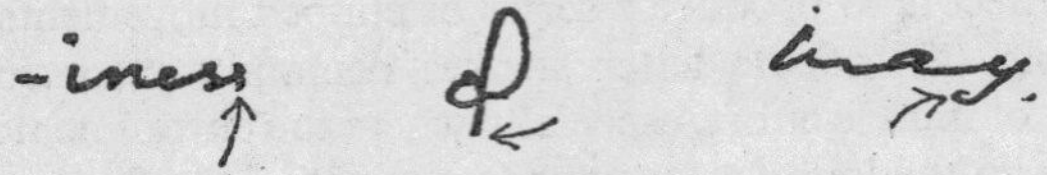

Fig. 22.

Examples of 'chopping off' which indicate emotional blockage in the handwriting

The Compulsive Writer

Many of us indulge in small pieces of compulsive behaviour. We may walk down a pavement and try to avoid the cracks, or tell ourselves that something pleasant will happen if the traffic lights change by the time we reach them. In psychology such behaviour is called 'undoing'. It is relatively normal and commonplace.

The truly compulsive individual, however, makes a ritual out of many of the most trivial aspects of life. This can be seen as an anxiety-reducing strategy which helps a person with emotional problems to cope by keeping them constantly busy. However, the compulsive behaviour itself is not especially helpful and may drastically hinder everyday living. Compulsive hand-washers for example, may be constantly cleaning and scrubbing at their fingers in an attempt to scour away imagined grime.

The compulsive person, like those who curtail their emotions, does so because he, or she, finds the free expression of feelings distasteful. However, while emotional constipation is a general but mild defence against anxiety-arousing emotions, the compulsive individual wages an all-out war against them.

The essence of their behaviour can be summed up in one word – *repetition*. If, for example, they are faced with solving a problem which arouses anxiety, they will attempt to do so by constant and repetitive efforts. These will be maintained even if the problem turns out to be insoluble.

Such an exaggerated determination may sound admirable and, indeed, the compulsive person is often regarded as conscientious by others. But their approach to life is fraught with difficulties, as the problem-solving strategies adopted are rigid and stereotyped. They find it extremely difficult to look at problems from a fresh angle or to consider different methods of approach. This applies no matter what difficulty they are trying to resolve, from a problem at work to one involving human relationships. Even when it becomes obvious that the method is not going to work, the compulsive individual continues to use it. Often not from any real belief in their ultimate success but because anxieties are reduced as long as an effort is being made. Thus the problem-solving procedure is not a rational attempt to reach a solution but a defence reaction.

An example of such compulsive behaviour is the refusal of one partner in a broken relationship to accept that the affair is over and to persist in phoning, calling and writing. An emotionally balanced individual might try this tactic for a short period, but the truly compulsive person will continue for months and even years. The person usually realises that such behaviour is irrational but is unable to give it up for fear of being engulfed by emotions. The repeated attempts to 'win back' their partner's affections help to keep the distress and anxiety caused by the break-up at a tolerable level.

The important difference between compulsive and persistent activities is that the person with a compulsion frequently carries his or her behaviour to bizarre extremes, which often makes him appear odd or eccentric. Typical compulsions are checking the doors and windows a prescribed number of times each night, even though one check would be sufficient for reasons of security; having strong urges, which are rarely carried through, to do something 'bad'; worrying about 'bad' thoughts for fear they will come true; checking and rechecking every piece of work to avoid any possibility of a mistake. All these, and the many other forms of compulsive behaviours in which people indulge might be summed up under the heading of 'not being able to leave well enough alone'.

Compulsive behaviours may be merely an inconvenience or they may prove so overpowering that they come to dominate an individual's existence and therapeutic help has to be sought.

The handwriting characteristics described below will allow you to detect the presence of a compulsion and determine its seriousness. If they start to appear in your own handwriting you should treat them as a warning to take life rather less seriously, to strive less for perfection, precision and order and to relax more often.

Signs of Compulsion in Handwriting

Letter Stutter
This refers to the accidental repetition of letters in a word or of strokes when forming a letter. Notice the word 'seem' in the example below. It has been written with three 'e's. The writer was unable to stop forming loops. The same unnecessary repetition is shown below where the letter 'm' has been given an additional loop.

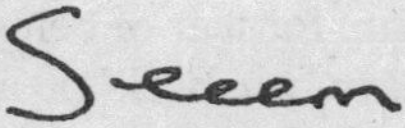

Fig. 23.

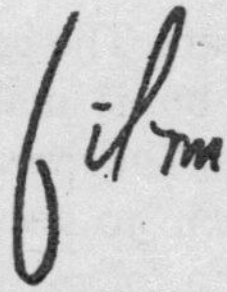

Fig. 24.

Although a letter stutter which appears once in a sample could be highly significant, it might equally be a slip of the pen. But stutters which occur twice or more are important indications of a compulsive emotional problem.

Repeated 'i' dots or 't' crosses
Double 'i' dots, and additional cross-strokes on 't's illustrated below are indications of compulsive behaviour, since the writer cannot resist repeating each action.

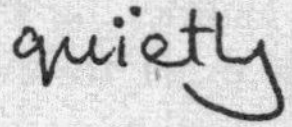

Fig. 25.

reports

Fig. 26.

Overwriting

Notice the way in which the letters in the examples below have been traced over again and again. The writer is anxious about making the message clear and so strives, counter-productively, for greater clarity.

Fig. 27.

Compulsive Additions

The writer adds strokes which improve neither the legibility nor the aesthetic look of the letters. This usually occurs in the upper or lower loops as an added extension. The compulsive additions have been arrowed in the examples below.

Fig. 28.
Added upper and lower extension

Fig. 29.
Added endstrokes

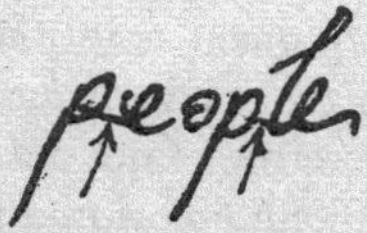

Fig. 30.
Added connective strokes

Added strokes occur because the writer, in a typical example of compulsive behaviour, refuses to leave the letters alone. Even though the original version was perfectly legible, the writer has been unable to resist adding some little extra to them in a futile attempt at greater perfection.

In addition to the signs described above, you should watch out for the sign of rigidity, curtailment and lateral pressure already described in this and previous chapters. Although not in themselves an indication of compulsivity, they represent a secondary trend which will add confirmation to your analysis. Most people with this form of emotional problem will have handwriting which is more or less rigid and many use curtailments and lateral pressure.

Because the above signs are rather unusual, and occur as a direct but unnecessary effort on the part of the writer, they may be regarded as significant even though you find only one or two examples in the handwriting sample. Any use of them should make you consider that the writer may be more or less compulsive and the greater their frequency the more serious this compulsive behaviour will be. The only exception may be letter stutter where, as we mentioned earlier, a pen slip might have been responsible. As with other handwriting signs, those related to emotional problems may appear temporarily in the handwriting of somebody going through a period of crisis, such as a bereavement, the loss of a valued relationship or some other major event likely to arouse deep and distressing feelings. You will probably have noticed that, when writing under anxiety-producing conditions, such as taking an examination, your script deteriorates somewhat, becoming more laboured, uncoordinated and unintelligible.

Anyone who manages to survive such a period without permanent emotional damage will find their writing reverts to normal as the trauma passes. By analysing handwriting you can, therefore, find out whether that person is passing through a difficult emotional period. This can be very important to understanding not only your own feelings but the nature of changes in relationships between you and the writer. People often attempt to deceive themselves and others about the seriousness of their emotional disturbances, whether permanent or temporary.

But they cannot deceive their handwriting – nor anybody who has learned how to interpret those give-away emotional signs in the script.

Chapter Eight

Handwriting and Health

In many American and European hospitals a new diagnostic aid has taken its place alongside the X-ray machines, ECG monitors and brain-scanners. Unlike those costly and sophisticated items of equipment, however, this needs nothing more complex than a pen and a sheet of paper. And the only sample the patient has to provide is some handwriting. But if the requirements of the diagnosis are cheap and simple, the results have proved impressive. Very often it enables the accurate prediction of some serious illness far earlier than has proved possible with the most elaborate electronic and chemical techniques.

We have already seen how your writing is able to indicate many areas of emotional disturbance because of its power to preserve minute internal disharmonies caused by psychological difficulties. The same applies to physiological problems which frequently reveal themselves in the handwriting long before they could be detected by any other methods – and often before the writer is even aware of the disability.

Clinical studies have shown that handwriting analysis can help doctors in four main ways. It enables them to determine the risk of an individual contracting a serious illness or to assess the probability that such a condition already exists in the patient. It allows them to follow the development of a mental or physical health problem and, finally, provides a means of studying the effects of drugs on the course of the illness.

The value of such analysis as a diagnostic aid has been clearly established by studies in the United States funded by the American Cancer Society. After many years of investigations, which involved the testing of thousands of individuals, researchers have developed a technique for the detection and prediction of cancer based solely on handwriting samples. This has proved so effective that specialists can now detect cancer in its earlier stages with more than 90% accuracy and predict its presence with a remarkable 75% accuracy often years before a diagnosis is possible using any other technique. This alerts the patient to a possible risk and ensures that regular check-ups are carried out. If these confirm the presence of cancer at a later date it will have been detected at a far earlier stage than might otherwise have been possible. This allows treatment to begin at a time when it has the best possible chance of success.

Studies of handwriting are also proving invaluable in the area of mental health. In Germany, Professor H. J. Haase, one of Europe's most widely respected neurologists, uses this method of analysis to assess the effects of drugs on mental illnesses. He has found that handwriting provides a more immediate and sensitive indication of his patients' response to medication than does their actual behaviour.

In many other clinical areas, too, the new science of graphonomy is taking its place as a respected and reliable aid to diagnosis and treatment. With research projects into the medical uses of graphonomy continuing in hospitals and laboratories around the world, its importance seems certain to increase in the years to come.

You can put the discoveries already made to work in your own life as a means of simply but safely monitoring your mental and physical health. The only equipment necessary is that described in chapter two. But the procedures which you will be shown in this chapter are exactly the same as used by medical science.

The first area of health care we will look at, since its effects are so powerful and pervasive, is that of stress control.

Handwriting and Stress

In chapter three we described a test for stress danger levels which also enables one to predict the writer's most likely response to a stressful situation. There will, however, be many situations in which it is either impossible or inconvenient to use the carbon paper procedure discussed. For instance, you might want to make a quick check of your stress levels when carbon paper is unavailable or to assess somebody else's handwriting without their knowledge. Fortunately this can be done solely from a sample of script, since stress leaves an unmistakable spoor on the handwriting trail which can be easily detected by applying the techniques detailed in this chapter.

Excessive mental and/or physical stress produces chemical changes in muscle tissue which we experience as fatigue. By making these changes, and so creating a feeling of tiredness, the body is effectively switching on a safety valve. It is decreasing the efficiency of the muscles to ensure that less work can, or will, be done by them, thereby reducing the risk of damage through unacceptable levels of strain.

This reduced muscular efficiency inevitably produces a clearly detectable trace in the handwriting sample, since the writing muscles are just as affected by the chemical changes as any other parts of the body. Due to the extreme sensitivity of handwriting, however, this trace appears in your script well before it becomes apparent elsewhere.

HANDWRITING STRESS SIGNS

Fading

Notice how the starting and ending strokes of the letters below show a loss of pressure – indicated by the arrows.

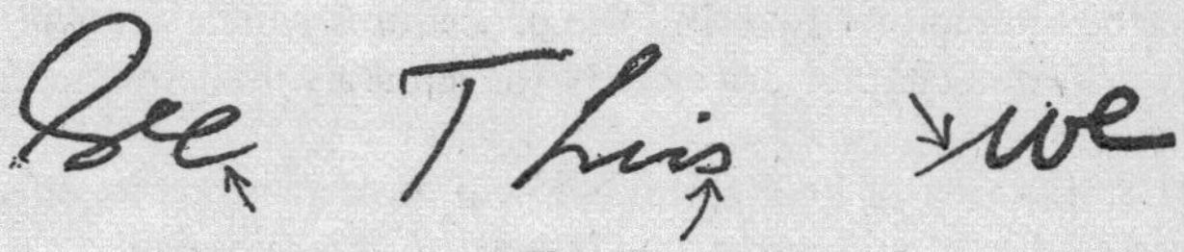

Fig. 1.

Fading at the start of a letter is due to the writer applying insufficient force until the pen-point was well into the stroke formation. Fading at the end of a letter is caused by a too rapid release of pressure. In both instances they reflect an inability on the part of the writer to sustain the necessary writing effort.

Faltering pressure, which is seen as fading, results from minute increases in fatigue in the more delicate of the writing muscles. These reflect the rising exhaustion when it is still at a very low level, long before its presence can be detected in the larger muscle groups.

Resting Dots

The arrows indicate a thickening in the strokes of the letters produced by the writer hesitating or 'resting' for a fraction of a second before moving the pen-point onwards. These 'rest pauses' are far too brief to be detected by the writers themselves or by anybody watching them write. But they are preserved in the script. As with fading the resting dots indicate fatigue in the writing muscles and thus warn that stress levels may be starting to rise unacceptably high.

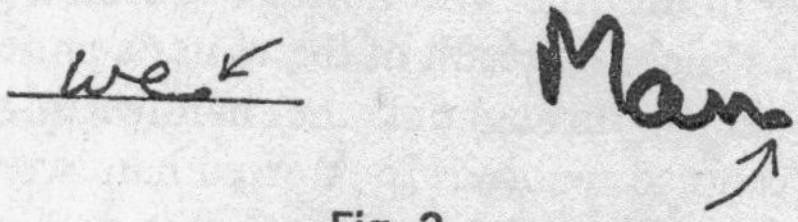

Fig. 2.
Resting Dots

Wavy Words

Sometimes normally-formed handwriting suddenly degenerates into a wavy, formless line which rather resembles a tidal mark on the sand. This is indicated by the arrow in the Example One below. You will see that less pressure has been used to form this stroke than appears in the rest of the world. As a result of the waviness the letter size has been reduced. This is a good indication of increasing stress, but you should be careful not to confuse waviness and letter reduction resulting from this type of difficulty with normal waviness and reduction which reflects a style of writing rather than a response to stress. Example Two shows a handwriting sample in which waviness and reduction are a normal feature of the script. Notice that the reduced areas are consistent in pressure and seem much less incongruous than the stress produced form.

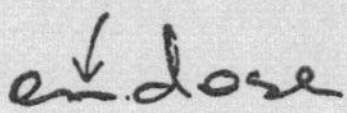

Fig. 3.

Example one — Waviness and letter reduction resulting
from stress

Fig. 4.

Example two — Waviness and letter reduction occurring
as a style of handwriting

So far as letter reduction is concerned, you can distinguish between normal and stress-induced changes by watching for three key differences:

1. Stress reduction in handwriting occurs sporadically and unpredictably in an otherwise normally formed script. Reduction of letters which is a result of the writer's preferred *style* will occur consistently throughout the handwriting and certain letters are *always* so reduced. In stressed handwriting reduction seems to occur without any pattern or purpose.

2. Most of the writing in *style*-produced letter reduction will appear rather unclearly formed. In stress-induced reduction, by contrast, many of the letters will appear carefully formed with only random instances of illegibility.

3. Finally, reduction in letters due to *style* of writing is accompanied by normal pressure throughout the script. Where reduction is caused by stress there will usually be an associated pressure loss.

Producing formless, wavy letters requires less muscular effort than those which have to be carefully formed. The tired, stressed writer is, therefore, very likely to slip into a wavy word form now and again with occasional letter deformation revealing this increasing inner fatigue.

Letter Lurches

Notice the sudden lurches (indicated by arrows) in the letter below. These usually occur on *upward and outward* movement when creating the rising stroke of ascenders or lines which, as in the case of the 'y' anchor stroke, rise above the writing line. This happens because outward and upward movements are produced using less pressure than downstrokes which are executed with increased pressure. This rhythmic waxing and waning pressure pattern of strokes was discussed in chapter three.

Because less pressure is used in the upward and outward stroke the pen is, momentarily, under less muscular control. This means that any decrease in the efficiency of the writing muscles, resulting from stress and fatigue, is most likely to affect this type of pen movement.

These lurches can, however, occur in downstrokes where levels of stress are serious. Despite the fact that the pen is under greater muscular control, and heavier pressure is being applied to form the stroke, there is a loss of guidance. Since the lapse has to reveal itself through a relatively greater degree of control and pressure, the muscular fatigue will clearly be all the greater. You should pay special attention to letter lurches which are present in downstrokes.

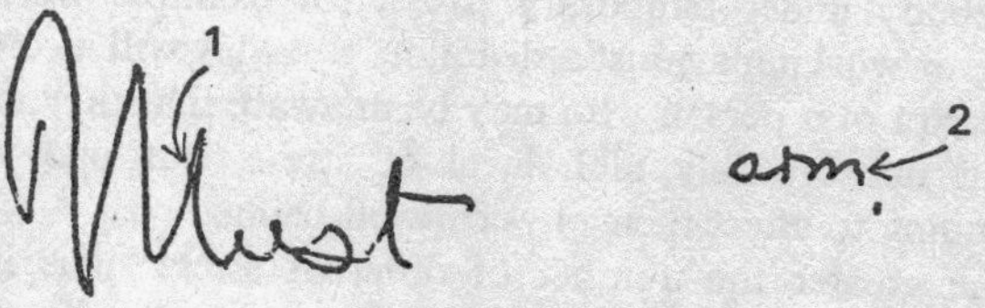

Fig. 5.
Letter lurches – notice the loss of pressure on the upward and outward stroke (arrow 1). More serious stress problems are indicated by a downward loss of control (arrow 2)

Broken Strokes

Letter lurches are not the only indication of serious stress levels to be detected in downstrokes. Notice the breaks (indicated by arrows) in the two examples below. There is a crack in the curve of the 'F' in February and in the letter 'I' (which has been magnified in order to make the break clearer) and there has been a complete failure of pressure. Although brief, it probably lasted less than 1/100th second. Such a total breakdown in pressure is highly significant since the downstrokes of letters are normally formed in one quick burst of motion.

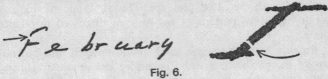

Fig. 6.

Letter Breaks in Strokes

These, then, are the five major indications of stress in handwriting:

1: Fading
2: Resting dots
3: Wavy words
4: Letter lurches
5: Broken downstrokes

They are very likely to be present in handwriting produced by somebody under temporary stress, for example when upset, tired, or working against a deadline. But they will also occur in the script of a person who may be unaware that they are living at an unacceptably high level of stress, but one which is beginning to affect their physical well-being.

The greater the number of different stress signs in handwriting and the more frequently they occur, the higher the levels of stress and the more serious the fatigue and internal strain.

Watch for these stress warnings in your own handwriting. If they start to become a permanent, rather than a temporary, feature of the script, carry out the more detailed stress check using the monitor described in chapter three. At the same time you should pause to reflect on those aspects of your lifestyle which may be causing long-term difficulties. Try to reduce them whenever possible, relax more frequently, check your diet and, perhaps, take more exercise. Stress can be highly beneficial when used correctly, as one of the current authors has described.* But if allowed to get out of control it will prove a major hazard to mental and physical health.

HANDWRITING AND THE HEAVY DRINKER

A frequent result of excessive daily stress levels is a desire to escape into the numbing comfort of alcohol. Most people enjoy the occasional drink, to relax with at the end of the day or when socialising with friends. There is certainly nothing wrong with this. In fact, a recent medical study in America has shown that those who drink in moderation are actually healthier and tend to live longer than complete abstainers. However, when the levels of stress are especially high, and you feel harassed, tense, lonely, depressed or frustrated, social drinking can easily get out of hand and develop into a serious and harmful problem.

Physical changes produced by even moderate amounts of alcohol can usually be readily detected in the handwriting. In fact it is such an accurate indicator that the police in Sweden and the United States, as well as taking blood or urine samples, examine the handwriting of people suspected of drunken driving. In several recent court cases it has been the handwriting samples, analysed for the court by forensic experts, which have been the deciding factor in securing a conviction.

There are two effects of alcohol which have the most profound influence on handwriting. The first is a lowering of concentration, the second an impairment of the flow of messages from brain to muscles. This means that the disorganised higher centres of the brain attend less effectively to the writing task and transmit their commands less efficiently. Because the movements needed to form letters are so precise and subtle they are among the first to reflect these alcohol-induced disturbances.

The changes they produce are remarkably consistent between different writers, as several major studies have shown. One such investigation was carried out, using a large group of subjects, by Dr. Neils Riesby at the University of Copenhagen in Denmark. Not only was he able to establish that, although drink affects

* *Thrive on Stress,* Dr. Robert Sharpe and David Lewis, Souvenir Press.

many aspects of behaviour differently in different people, there is a distinct pattern to handwriting variations under the influence of alcohol.

This type of analysis can help you detect and monitor serious drink difficulties in yourself or somebody close to you. At a more immediate level of health preservation, it can also help to tell whether you, or a friend, are over the legal limit for alcohol when driving. If you are at a party and find that your handwriting fails the 'Scriptalyser' tests described below, you can also be certain that it will fail the breathalyser test if you are pulled up by the police.

How Alcohol Alters your Handwriting

Under the influence of alcohol a person's behaviour becomes both more exaggerated and more variable. For example speech grows slurred yet increases in range and volume; walking becomes an elaborate, if uncertain, caricature of the sober gait; grasping and lifting objects takes on an air of pantomime. Handwriting is similarly affected, becoming more extravagant but far less consistent.

There are marked changes in handwriting pressure, which increases but becomes increasingly variable. The writing expands and becomes less regular. Letters generally show an increase in height, usually by as much as 20% or more, but become far more uneven. They also get wider and show greater variation in width than is found in the handwriting of sober individuals.

Relaxation of the writing muscles results in a script which has a limp appearance due to decreased firmness in the forward writing impulse. Just as we generally talk of people becoming 'weak willed' as a result of drinking so too can the graphonomist talk of their writing becoming 'weak worded', with a marked loss of drive as the muscles start to relax.

It is important to appreciate that people differ in the response to alcohol not only in their general levels of tolerance but from one situation to another. The effects on the brain and nervous system will be determined by a whole range of factors, including mood and how recently a meal was eaten. This means that the relaxation of the muscles and the progressive careless-ness in the formation of letters will occur at different speeds from one occasion to the next. As alcoholic influence increases the writer makes less and less attempt to produce a clear style which would overtax the already ill-controlled muscles. Letters become increasingly illegible, 'o's and 'a's are less carefully closed, 't' cross-strokes may be left off and other strokes remain unfinished.

How to Scriptalyse your Handwriting

You have been drinking at a party and now want to drive home. You feel fine and perfectly in control. This, as any doctor or policeman will tell you, can be a dangerously deceptive state. How can you tell whether or not you are safe to drive? Clearly if you *know* that you have drunk more than the legal limit there is no doubt about the matter. You cannot and should not get behind the wheel of your car. But there are many occasions when you have drunk within the limit but still worry that perhaps, on this occasion, your responses might have been dangerously slowed down. One way of checking is by giving your handwriting the written equivalent of the breath test. Here is how you scriptalyse your writing. Jot down a few lines, study the results and then answer the following six questions.

Does your handwriting . . .

1: Grow taller and more variable in height?

2: Grow wider and more variable in width?

3: Grow heavier and more variable in pressure? (This can be checked by reference to chapter three and the Pressure Pad if you want to make absolutely certain.)

4: Become limp, with less firmness in its forward motion?

5: Show reduced definition of the letter stroke so that they are harder to read?

6: Show a marked increase in errors, of spelling, writing the wrong letters, and especially mistakes caused by letter or stroke transposition?

If you answered *yes* to two or more questions the probability is that your blood alcohol level is above the safe legal limit to drive a car. You should certainly not attempt to do so.

But it is important to understand that even if the above changes are not noticeable in your handwriting this is no guarantee that you are fit to drive. It is possible that some aspect of your tolerance for alcohol, body weight or muscle co-ordination have delayed the onset of the symptoms listed here. However, one can say for certain that where they are present you should not drive a car.

The three examples of handwriting shown here will help you to identify some of the major differences between sober and intoxicated writing. They were produced as part of our own research project – for which we found no shortage of volunteers! The subjects were given measured amounts of alcohol and then asked to write the same sentence at different levels of drunkenness.

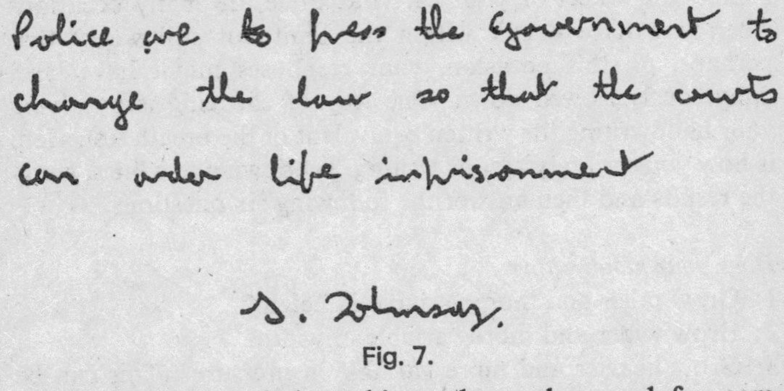

Police are to press the Government to change the law so that the courts can order life imprisonment

J. Johnson.

Fig. 7.

The handwriting of the subject when sober used for comparison. Notice that the script is fairly small and the pressure reasonably even.

The second sample was produced after the subject had three drinks. At this point he was asked to fill out a questionnaire to determine his confidence in his ability to competently write, walk and drive a car. Although well above the legal limit he was convinced that he could drive safely. Scriptalysing his hand-

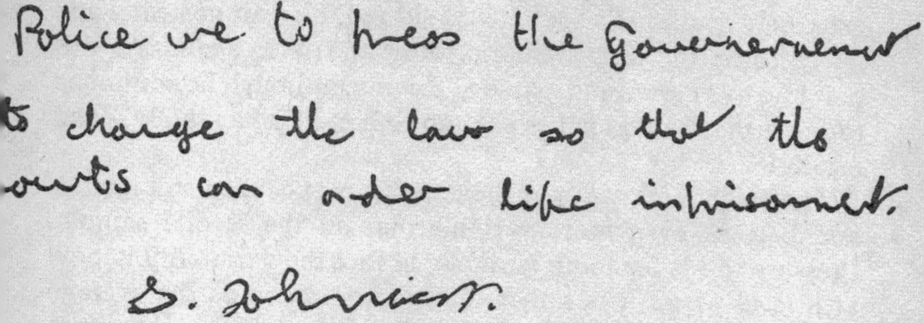

Fig. 8

writing might have convinced him that he was far from sober enough to drive. Note that the letters have become both taller and broader, and that they have become far more variable in these dimensions. Compare this sample with Figure 7 to see this variability especially clearly. Pressure is far more variable than in the first sample as well. Compare the word 'to' in the first line with the word 'to' in the second line. The writing has become slacker as well. Notice especially the changes in the signature.

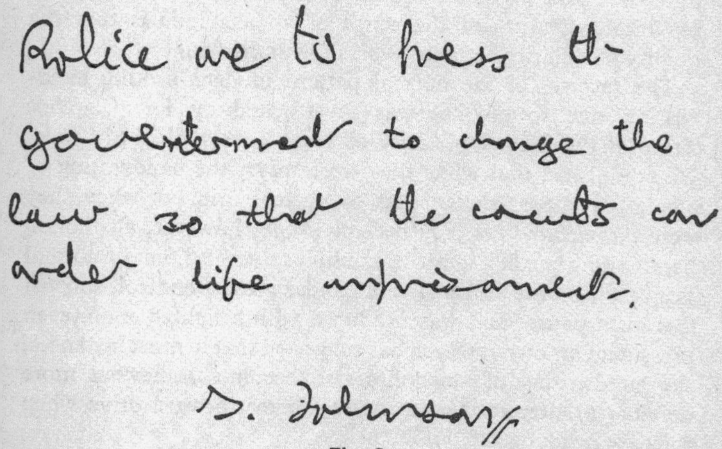

Fig. 9.

The sample in Figure 9 was obtained when the writer was

extremely drunk. His speech was slurred, his gait unsteady and he repeated the same remarks over and over again. At this point he was clearly incapable of driving, although he continued to insist that he was sober enough to handle a car safely – and legally!

The height and width of the letters has expanded still further and become even more variable than in the second sample. Pressure too is far more variable, in fact the variability is now at a level where it is rather difficult to determine the average pressure at all, a trend which was already becoming apparent in the second sample. Letter form is less definitive and there has been a mistake, and clumsy attempt at correction, in the formation of the word 'government' (line 2). Further slackness can be observed, again this is very obvious in the signature.

By making this sort of comparison it is possible to determine approximately how much the writer has been drinking and how alcohol affects him. The young volunteer who wrote those samples was a student who drank only occasionally. Had he suffered from a serious drinking problem, however, a completely different result would have been obtained from the test. For a remarkable feature of the script of an alcoholic is that the quality and clarity actually *improve* with drinking.

The reversal of the normal pattern of deteriorating handwriting due to alcohol was investigated by Dr. Clarence Tripp at the State University of New York's Alcohol Clinic. He established that when they were *sober*, the handwriting of alcoholics appeared like that of normal drinkers when they were *intoxicated*! As they became *drunk*, however, alcoholics' handwriting steadily improved until it resembled that of normal drinkers who are *sober*. It came under greater control, showed less disturbance, and was produced with a lighter, more even pressure. Our own research has suggested that in most instances, the handwriting of alcoholics also becomes somewhat more definite in letter form and shows greater forward drive when they are drinking.

When an individual's motor-control improves with rising levels of intoxication he, or she, has crossed the physical and mental threshold of alcohol dependence. Now drinking is no longer an impediment to effective behaviour but an essential requirement for it.

If you suspect that somebody has a drinking problem, simply compare handwriting samples taken when they are sober and again after a few drinks. Look for the following changes between the scripts.

1: Pressure decreases
2: Pressure becomes more regular
3: Mistakes, disturbances decrease
4: The handwriting becomes more definite with more distinct letter formation.
5: Handwriting acquires more forward drive, loses flaccidity and slackness.

As with other activities, the amount of alcohol needed to bring about an improvement in overall control varies considerably from one person to the next. In some alcoholics it takes only one or two 'steadying drinks' to bring about the changes we have described.

If some or all of these changes occur under the influence of alcohol, the writer is very likely to have a drink problem and should seek treatment or help in overcoming the dependency.

HANDWRITING AND PHYSICAL ILLNESS

In one of the longest and most intensive studies of the link between handwriting and physical illness ever attempted, Drs. Daniel Casten and Alfred Kanfer of New York, investigated the case histories and analysed the writing of more than 10,000 seriously ill Americans. Their massive investigation, funded by grants from the American Cancer Society, resulted in the development of screening tests, based on an examination of handwriting, which are now used in many US hospitals. In addition to their association with cancer, these signs have also been observed in the writing of patients in the early stages of various heart diseases and other serious ailments.

Here we want to look at some of these indications in a

person's script which reveal early signs of such physical disabilities as cancer and heart disease.

When studying handwriting as a guide to assessing the writer's health, your starting point is the pressure used. As we have already explained, healthy handwriting has a rhythmic ebb and flow of pressure, with heavier pressure on the downstrokes alternating with lighter pressure on the upstrokes.

In the magnified sample of script below, this normal pressure pattern is indicated by the arrows. You will see that less pressure has been used when forming the upward strokes (arrows 1, 2, 3) than on the downstrokes (4, 5, 6). Notice also that where the stroke curves to form the junction between up- and downstrokes (arrows 7, 8, 9) the change is smooth and gradual. The lines sweep around without hesitation.

Fig. 10.
Pressure pattern in normal handwriting

The sample below illustrates another aspect of the healthy handwriting style, the gradual transition from thick to thin stroke in the loops of letters. In the letter 'h' observe how the

Fig. 11.
Normal handwriting produces letters which have
a gradual transition from thick to thin strokes

upstroke is lighter and changes smoothly into the downstroke at the top of the loop. Similarly with the letter 'o', there is heavier pressure on the left side than on the right, but the transition is gradual and effortless from thick to thin line.

It is important to identify these indications of the healthy writing flow because when analysing script for the characteristics of serious illness you will be seeking out departures from this smooth, rhythmic stroke formation and pressure pattern. The departures from this normal style are the result of an irregular transmission of signals from the brain to the muscles involved in writing. Although the exact nature of their influence is not yet known, it has been established that they are associated with certain types of serious illness and rarely occur otherwise.

The Signs of Physical Illness

The samples of handwriting which illustrate this section of the book are based on words written with a nib pen. *They will not show up in a biro or fibre-tip script.* The best type of pen to use for this form of analysis is the dip type which is still used in some old-fashioned post offices. This rather crude-looking pen has a split steel nib, attached to a wooden handle, which is ideal for showing up pressure variations and changes in stroke flow. You may, however, use fountain-pen samples when necessary, since the signs described below can often be detected in this form of writing. Also, use a good quality bond writing paper when possible.

Stiff Bends and Sudden Changes

The first sign to look out for is an abrupt change from a down- to an upstroke. Compare the example below with the normal writing in the sample above. Notice how the smooth transition from a downward to an upward stroke movement is missing and there has been a loss of pressure in the upstroke.

A crucial point to consider is the comparison between the thickness of the two strokes. If the downwards line is four or more times thicker than the upwards line a serious health problem may be present.

Fig. 12.
An inability to corner correctly results in a sudden upshoot. The comparison of down- and upstroke widths (indicated by arrows) is a key factor

This departure from normal handwriting is caused by the writer's inability to exert the fine muscle control required to corner smoothly and gradually. Instead of gliding around the bend in the letter, the pen-point appears to have been jerked upwards, resulting in the sharp stroke, and then lost energy with a resulting decrease in pressure.

Similar stiff bends and sudden changes are also seen, occasionally, in the loops of letters, as shown below.

Fig. 13.

Stroke Stiffness – Uniform Pressure
Look carefully at the illustrations below and notice how the 'm' has taken on a uniform shape, without clearly defined up- and downstrokes. There is a dull, even pressure throughout and the rhythmic flow which is characteristic of healthy handwriting has vanished. This can also be seen in the circular letters illustrated below. In addition these letters themselves become stiff and angular (indicated by arrows in Figure 15).

These changes indicate a degeneration in the writer's fine muscle co-ordination.

Fig. 14.

Shapeless form with
uniform stroke widths

Fig. 15.

The circular loopings are large,
of uniform width and having a
stiff, angular form

Segmentation in the writing

In chapter one, when describing the case history of Michael, the
executive under pressure, we discussed a feature of stroke
formation called segmentation. This is usually a sensitive early
warning sign of health dangers ahead. Notice how, in the
example below, the stroke has been chopped up so that minute
blobs of ink forming the letter appear like oblong beads
threaded on a necklace.

Fig. 16.

Segmentation, shown by arrows,
in a magnified portion of script

Segmentation is caused by tiny tremors of the writing muscles
which are transformed into up and down movement on the
paper. This clearly distinguishes it from gross tremors, present
in the writing of some elderly people, which produce a side-to-
side shake.

This is an important handwriting health sign and has been

found to indicate serious illness. Drs. Casten and Alfred Kafner found that it represents a later development in serious illness than that indicated by the stiff bends and sudden changes described above. However, the frequency of segmentation is an important factor in determining the extent of the health problem. In chapter one we explained that, since Michael's handwriting showed only a few such signs, he was advised to have regular medical checks. These finally identified a heart condition which could have been serious had it not been detected at an early stage. So, if you discover segmentation in handwriting it would be a sensible precaution to have a medical check-up as soon as possible. However, you must not become depressed or anxious, nor convince yourself that you are suffering from a serious and untreatable illness.

Bear in mind that the signs here, although shown to be closely associated with serious illness, *do not offer any sort of medical diagnosis*. What they do indicate is an increased *risk* of future health problems and provide a warning that some attention needs to be paid to this aspect of your life.

If the above signs appear in your handwriting and you also notice that it is becoming irregular in size and letter-spacing, the warning is slightly more urgent since these serve to underline the significance of the other indications.

In addition to sounding an early alarm on problems such as heart disease and cancer, handwriting has been shown to predict a wide range of other serious health difficulties. There are four key signs to watch out for:

1: Stroke tacking
2: Ink trails
3: Scatter dots
4: Sudden upshoot

All these occur in the handwriting sample opposite which was produced by a woman suffering from a severe lung condition. Look first at the letter 'b' in the word 'Sahib' and the 'k' in 'takes'. Notice that the final stroke of the 'b' has been formed with two lines rather than one at the stroke indicated by

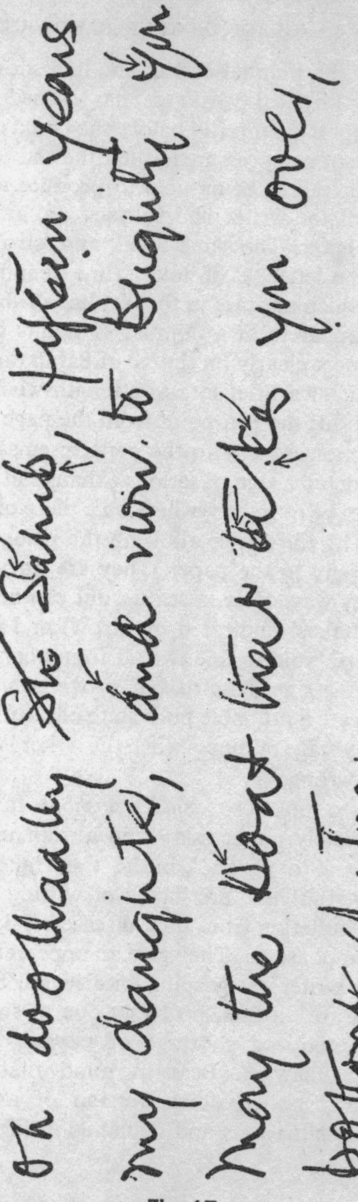

Fig. 17.

the arrow, where the pointed end of the line shows a sudden loss of strength. Physical weakness has caused the writing muscles to 'give up' momentarily before she could complete the letter. This failure of pen pressure has left the end of the broken stroke tapered. Instead of being able to produce a single continuous movement the writer had to 'tack on' another stroke to finish off the letter. The same break and 'stroke tack' can also be seen in the letter 'k' of 'takes' (line 3) and in the letter 'm' of 'bottom' which appears in the last line of the example.

Ink trails are apparent at a number of points in the script, but can be seen most clearly on the 'S' of Sahib (arrowed). The 'trail' is the result of a brief loss of strength where the writer was 'too weak' to lift the pen-point from the page, and instead let it drop back momentarily to the paper prematurely. Again this can be considered a sign of serious exhaustion.

Scatter dots can be found anywhere on a piece of paper, since they are formed by the writer allowing the pen-point to drop suddenly and briefly to the paper. They are not connected to the writing in any way. Here, a scatter dot can be seen behind the letter 'k' in 'takes' (indicated by arrow) and in the cup of the 'y' in the word 'you' in line two. If found consistently in a sample, these three signs, the *tacked stroke*, *scatter dots*, and the *ink trail* indicate a probable poor state of health. They often appear at an early stage of illness when the writer is still unaware that anything is wrong.

The final sign to look for is *sudden upshoot*. In the example, notice the completely unnecessary and abrupt upward movements in the 'a' and 'd' of 'and', in the 't' of 'takes' and the 'b' of 'boat' (arrowed). These are lapses of writing control often found in people suffering from lung diseases: TB, pleurisy and as in this case, emphasema. They give an appearance of breathlessness, as if the writer was gasping for air while the stroke was being made and are, in fact, probably due to sudden, minute and otherwise unnoticed shortage of oxygen of which the writer remained unaware. Bear in mind that handwriting provides a greatly scaled down version of an individual's response to other situations and demands in life. A weakness in the script is the first indication of a more general weakness which will, unless checked, eventually be large and damaging enough to appear in more obvious ways. If a persistent disturbance occurs in your own handwriting, or that of a close friend or relative, be on the alert for further physical symptoms. Should they occur it would be wise to seek medical advice. Be careful, however, to distinguish between short-term weaknesses which produce temporary changes in handwriting and the permanent indications which warn of more lasting health problems.

Before leaving this subject we would like to stress that handwriting signs do *not* provide a *diagnosis* of illness – only your doctor can do that. All the research has clearly established is that they are highly reliable early warning signals.

HANDWRITING AND MENTAL HEALTH

Mental and physical health are not opposite sides of the same coin. They are closely interconnected aspects of overall well-being, since there is invariably a physical involvement in mental illness and a mental component in physical distress. Furthermore it is now well established that mental difficulties are often the cause of seemingly independent bodily ailments. Heart disease, cancer, ulcers and liver ailments, for example, have been found to be more common in some types of personality than in others. This is an important point to consider when analysing handwriting for the indications of mental health.

The script signs we shall be describing here do not invariably indicate the presence of a specific mental problem but are general characteristics of writing that research has shown are frequently linked to this form of illness.

You will find these interpretations useful should you be concerned about your own health, but even more importantly if somebody close to you is showing symptoms which would seem to indicate a mental disturbance.

Some of the most valuable work in this area has been undertaken by Dr. Donald Douglas, chief neurologist at the Lenox Hill Hospital in New York. He has shown that a number of handwritings can be positively linked to mental health problems since they are hardly ever found in the handwriting of mentally normal writers. Our own research, with a large sample of neurotic, schizophrenic and acutely depressed patients support the findings. The major handwriting indications of mental ill-health are as follows:

Change to Childlike Script

This occurs in the handwriting of many mentally ill people, often from the very start of their difficulties. The samples below show what happens as the individual's normal writing begins, slowly but surely, to resemble that of a child. This change is consistent with the regression to childlike behaviour often associated with mental illness. The patient cannot come to terms with the pressures, responsibilities and stresses of life as an adult and so begins to revert back to a state of childlike dependence. The regression is a gradual process but one which becomes increasingly pronounced as the illness grows more serious.

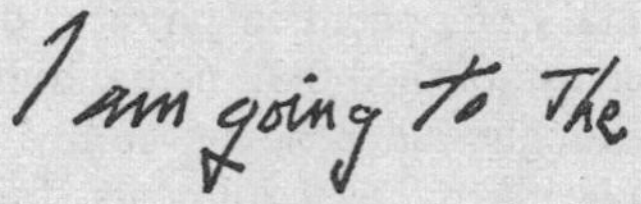

I am going to The

Fig. 18.
Sample of handwriting from man aged 43 shortly
before the onset of mental illness

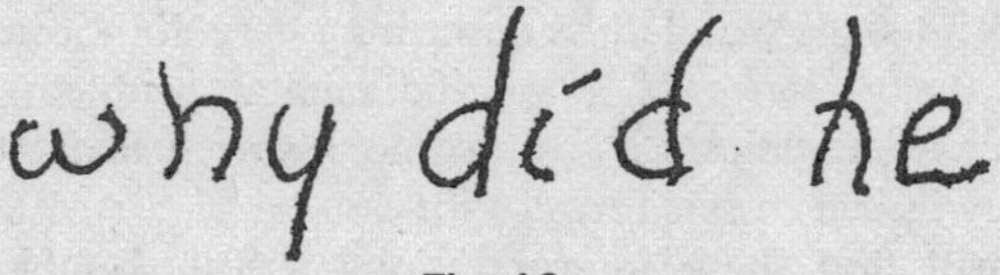

why did he

Fig. 19.
Change in handwriting of same man after
he had become mentally ill

Distortion of Individual Letters
In the sample below the arrows indicate where distortion has occurred in the individual letters. This is most probably caused

by the writer being unable to attend sufficiently to the task in hand, a deficiency which is often associated with mental illness. In order to create the letter forms shown, the writer had to produce uncontrolled and exaggerated movements of the pen.

Fig. 20.

Abnormal Contraction and Expansion of Letters
Notice the variations in size of the letters in the sample of handwriting below. Some of them are quite large, others have shrunk down to little more than a line. Such gross size differences are rarely found in the handwriting of normal individuals but occur frequently in the writing of psychotic subjects.

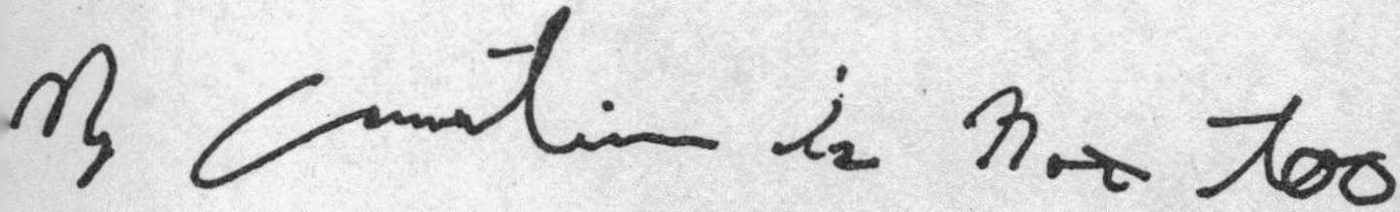

Fig. 21.

Extreme Disturbance of the Writing Line
Notice the changes and irregularity in the direction of the writing line in the sample below. Research has shown that such lines wobble, which is caused by a failure of attention on the part of the writer, is frequently linked to mental problems.

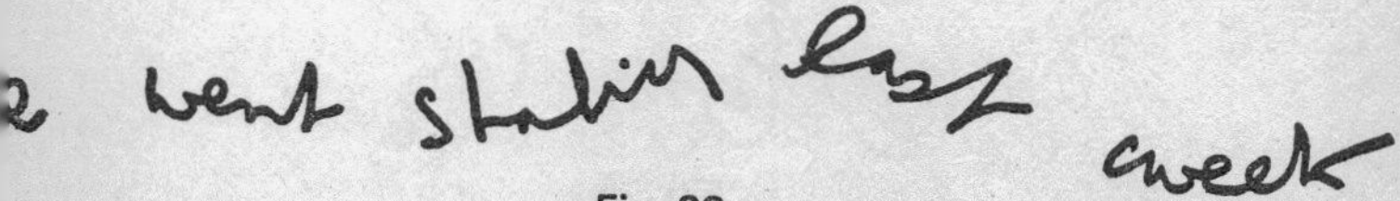

Fig. 22.

Letter Splitting

This sign occurs when, for no reason, the writer splits his letter forms in half. The arrows indicate these splits in the example below. This seems to symbolise the splitting of the writer's emotional and intellectual world into two distinct entities, a separation frequently observed in the mentally ill.

Fig. 23.

Blurred and Blotched Handwriting

The ink smears in the example shown below was not done with the fingers, but occurred spontaneously as the writing was produced. It is caused by loss of control of the pen pressure.

Fig. 24.

Bizarre Letter Forms

These are weird embellishments which the writer adds to letters in an attempt to draw attention to the script. This desire for their writing to stand out is consistent with the lack of self-esteem experienced by many mentally ill people. The additions to letters often take the form of elaborate loops and whorls, as shown in the example below.

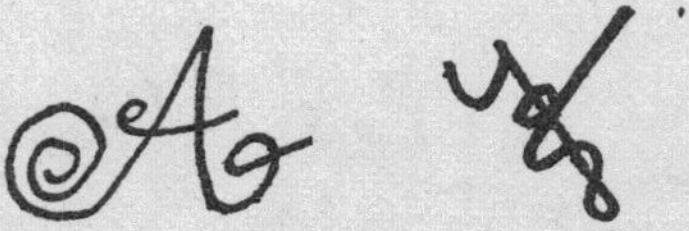

Fig. 25.

If even *one* of the above signs is present in the handwriting sample you are analysing, it suggests some form of mental disturbance. To be significant, however, the sign – or signs – must occur more than once and persist in the writing over a period of time as their occasional use might be due to a slip of the pen and have no special meaning.

As with all the handwriting characteristics described in this and other chapters, bear in mind that frequency and consistency are always associated with the increasing seriousness of the internal condition responsible for them.

Before leaving this chapter we would like to stress one further point. It is well known that many medical students, during training, are convinced they are suffering from most of the diseases they study! The same may be said of every reader of a home medical dictionary. A brief glance through the lists of symptoms and pages of diseases is usually sufficient to convince even the healthiest and most balanced individual that all is not well with them. Somebody who is already anxious and fearful of their health can easily come to believe that their time has come. Because simply reading about an illness, especially a serious one, is sufficient to convince a few people they are its victims, no responsible author enters lightly into the medical arena.

However, simply to ignore this important area of handwriting research would, it seems to us, be quite unacceptable. The early and reliable prediction of serious illness is an aspect of medical investigation of vital importance to all of us. All too often it is only because major physical and mental illness is *not* identified at a sufficiently early stage that treatment proves difficult and possibly ineffective. If the development of handwriting analysis leads doctors to an improvement in early diagnostic accuracy then it will have played a major role in raising health standards and preventing unnecessary suffering.

The studies which have formed the basis of this chapter are a serious and important contribution to an understanding of the mind and body. If you are interested in the original sources of the material used here, they are listed in the bibliography.

If you decide to use handwriting analysis to explore your own or anybody else's health then please bear these essential points in mind:

* They only indicate risk, they do not diagnose. Leave that task to those who are qualified to form an expert opinion.

* No test is ever 100% reliable. This applies to every known method of clinical diagnosis. Handwriting has proved more accurate than other methods in several areas of diagnosis but even a 90% reliability means that, in ten cases out of a hundred, a mistake will occur.

* Finally, if you discover some of the signs we have described here in your own handwriting, do not become anxious and convinced that you are seriously ill. Check your writing over a periods of days or weeks. If they persist and if your lifestyle is such that it might be producing health problems – for example if you are working under a high level of long-term stress – then have a complete medical check. Such routine examinations are a good idea in any event after middle age, and of particular value if you are overweight, take little exercise and are in a generally run-down condition.

Chapter Nine

Handwriting and the Child

Handwriting analysis provides caring adults with a window onto the world of the child. By using the procedures of graphonomy, parents, teachers and all those concerned with the welfare of children, can obtain valuable insights which might not be made available to them by any other means. The accurate interpretation of youngster's handwriting enables us to explore their general development; to identify and thereby encourage the growth of creativity; and to understand their personalities and problems better so as to become more effective in guiding them through the emotional traumas of growing-up. These techniques have proved so revealing and reliable that they now form an essential part of educational assessment in Scandinavia, Germany, France, Holland and many parts of the United States.

In this chapter we will be explaining how you should set about analysing the handwriting of children, what you may discover and how this new knowledge can best be used to help the child. We will discuss the meaning of poor handwriting and consider two major styles of illegibility related to emotional difficulties. We will look at the very different problems associated with over- and under-development and describe how to diagnose them from handwriting. The assessment of behaviour through writing will be explained and we will show how the anxieties, frustrations and terms of the growing child are reflected in handwriting.

WHY HANDWRITING MATTERS SO MUCH

Which is more important – the appearance of a child's handwriting or what is written?

You may feel that content matters and that the script, so long as it can actually be read, is much less significant. After all, the first tells us about the child's imagination and level of intelligence, whereas legibility is merely a question of learning.

In theory at least this view is shared by the majority of adults. In a survey of 65 P.T.A. members we found 73% of parents and 87% of teachers answered that they would rate the originality of thought and creative expression of ideas far more highly than neatness and legibility in the script.

In practice their response is frequently the exact opposite. When it comes to the actual assessment of written work parents and, more especially teachers, place a strong emphasis on good handwriting. A child with a neat and legible style but negligible creativity will usually score higher marks and obtain better grades than the bright, creative youngster with poor handwriting. What is more, the neat writer will be seen as being *more* intelligent by teachers and *more* achieving by parents.

Of course, teachers usually deny this, so to explore the influence of legibility on teachers' assessment of school work, Dr. S. Soloff, a psychological researcher in the U.S., had the same essay copied out by neat and untidy writers. These were then marked by a number of teachers. Although the arguments and ideas were identical in every case, those essays copied out neatly received much higher marks and more favourable comments than the less legible versions. It was not a case of higher marks being awarded for neatness either. The comments made by teachers showed that ideas expressed very legibly were considered more appropriate, valid and praiseworthy. The result of this and other similar studies leaves no room for doubt about the importance of handwriting ability in the child. While adults may pay lip service to the criterion of originality in writing, the legibility and aesthetic appeal of the script also strongly influences their judgements.

The bright, imaginative child with poor writing skills will, therefore, often be penalised and frequently underrated. What might be done to improve this situation?

The first step is for parents and teachers to be aware that this prejudice exists. Only occasionally are adults perceptive enough about their own judgements to appreciate how presentation affects their attitudes. When reading the work of a child or adolescent we should attempt to separate what has been said from the way in which it has been set down on paper. We should not assume that a particular type of writing – perhaps our own – is superior to any other or that there is an 'ideal' aesthetic standard.

That having been said it cannot be denied that some writing is so poorly formed that one cannot simply ignore the lack of legibility. Nor would it be wise to do so. Research has shown that where the handwriting is highly illegible it indicates definite emotional problems on the part of the child.

It is important, before we go on to discuss what these emotional problems are and the signs you should look out for in order to discover such difficulties, to put legibility into a proper perspective.

Where writing ability is concerned, large differences can be found among children of all ages. This is to be expected since, as we have stressed throughout the book, writing is a uniquely personal form of self-presentation. It is only at a high level of illegibility, where the letter forms show the specific patterns and characteristics – which we will describe in a moment – that emotional problems are indicated.

In an investigation of the link between handwriting and social effectiveness, Dr. P. Oininen, of Finland's Jyvaskala University, tested a large number of children whose writing was rated into one of three categories – *poor*, *medium* and *good* – by their teachers. The children were also assessed on emotional stability, social skills and popularity. When the handwriting classifications were compared with the personality ratings, Dr. Oininen found a clear association between bad writing and ineffectiveness in other areas of life. Children with poor script were described by their teachers as being more than normally tense, finding it difficult to concentrate, and more disruptive in class. They tended to be less popular with their companions and to score higher on psychological tests for emotional disturbance. It is only fair to say, however, that the samples of handwriting categorised as 'poor' by Dr. Oininen's raters were especially illegible. Children whose writing is only slightly below average legibility could not be characterised by the behaviours listed above.

Our own research, which has included numerous interviews with British remedial handwriting teachers, strongly confirms Dr. Oininen's findings that serious illegibility is, to some considerable extent, a sign of emotional disturbance. In addition these children often have other learning difficulties so that their poor writing is only one of a number of problems.

If a child has very poor handwriting and is described by teachers in the terms applied to Dr. Oinonen's subjects, then professional help is usually indicated. There is a need for understanding and help in overcoming or resolving the emotional disturbances underlying the writing disability. It is very often hard for adults to admit that their own child could have a serious emotional difficulty, perhaps because such a diagnosis seems to reflect so badly on their abilities as parents. All too often attempts are made, either by the parents or the teachers, to improve the writing, as though this was the only problem to be solved. Threats, bribes, long hours of practice, sarcasm, mockery and even physical punishments are often the fate of the child with poor writing. Needless to say, such an approach can only make matters far worse by increasing anxiety and frustration, while eroding what is, typically, an already poor self-image.

A mistake which many teachers make is to brand a child's handwriting as illegible without trying to analyse exactly what makes it so poor, ugly or hard to read. It is often assumed, even by highly trained educators, that all handwriting problems can be tracked down to a single source. If that root cause of error is eliminated, the argument goes, then the illegibility will also disappear. Our own research has shown this is not what happens. There are a number of types of poor writing and different aspects of letter and word formation cause illegibility in the handwriting of different children. One child, for instance, may only write poorly because his letters are very variable in size and slant, another through insufficient fine muscle control which produces misshapen letters. In a third child it could be caused by a tense rigidity which means that he can only make straight lines and angles and cannot form curves.

We have frequently heard it said, by teachers and parents, that a child writes illegibly through a lack of effort: 'He simply does not try to produce neat words,' is a typical comment. This is almost always complete nonsense. Children with poor handwriting often show great concern, and become extremely frustrated, over the appearance of their script. They know it will be seen and judged by others. By adults whose love and respect they want to enjoy, and their companions whose ridicule they dread. They would dearly like to change their writing and exchange the harsh comments of parents and teachers for praise, but are unable – for a variety of reasons – to do so.

If you are a parent and concerned about the standard of your child's handwriting, you should understand that this is not something over which there is free choice. The child is not simply writing badly as an act of defiance or to annoy his teachers. Help with the emotional problems behind highly illegible handwriting must be given along with the usual remedial training. In the case of a child whose writing is poor but not dramatically so, sympathy and motivation to gradually improve legibility – within their own individual style – are the only effective tactics.

THE MEANING OF SPECIFIC FACTORS IN POOR HANDWRITING

Super-rigidity

This handwriting sample was produced by a fourteen-year-old

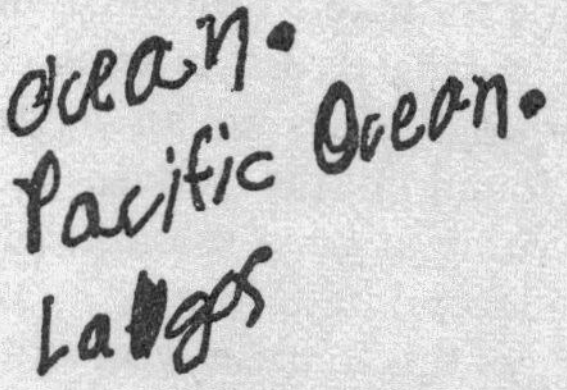

Fig. 1.

boy. It is striking in a number of ways and provides a graphic portrait of the youngster's personality.

Notice, for a start, that it is lacking in flow or fluency. The strokes appear tense, have been written with heavy pressure, and are extremely rigid. The writing is crowded and seems to resist forward movement towards the right side of the page. It has been held back by tension in the writing muscles.

By the time they are teenagers, most young people have acquired considerable handwriting fluency, but no such development is apparent here. The stiff and stilted writing movements make it difficult to form curves and the letters are extremely angular. Where a normal writer would form circles or ovals, this boy has used sharp corners.

This handwriting is characteristic of a tense, anxious and aggressive child, an interpretation emphasised by several other features in the script. The word 'Ocean' has its 'O' formed with an extra, unnecessary, double circle. A careful study also reveals that he has gone over and over the full-stops with such pressure that, on the original, it was found he had almost bored a hole in the paper in some places. These signs are similar to the indications of compulsiveness discussed in chapter seven and quite close in meaning. When combined with the relentless pressure exhibited by this writer, they reveal an aggressive and compulsive child who tends to use undue force or repeated resistance in an attempt to overcome problems or master difficult situations. His driving force is anxiety, an impression confirmed by the heavily crossed out mistake in the word 'Lagos'. He has pressed down hard on the pen, going backwards and forwards over the error, until it was obliterated. This desire to cover up a mistake so ruthlessly indicates resentment and anxiety over making errors in areas of school work apart from the handwriting. Clues to an aggressive and anxious nature are also found in the sudden increases in pressure throughout the writing, a good example of which can be seen in the 'a's in 'Pacific' and in 'Ocean'.

The handwriting of this fourteen-year-old would undoubtedly be judged as 'poor' by many adults. It is difficult to read and very likely to lead to damaging assessments of the child's intellectual development and abilities. How can such a writer best be helped?

An in-depth analysis of his handwriting suggests that the most appropriate method will combine understanding and sympathy, coupled with practical assistance over social difficulties. From his script, the child appears to be aggressive and may behave in such a way as to earn the label 'stubborn'. But the handwriting, while suggesting these traits, also provides clear evidence of inner doubts and fears. The writing indicates a child as anxious as he is aggressive. There is little point in concentrating on – and probably punishing – outbursts of aggression, which should be regarded as an indication of inner uncertainty about abilities. The focus of these fears may well be school work, but they are likely to have spread to other aspects of the boy's life; relationships at home and with friends, popularity among companions, self-image and hopes for the future. His poor handwriting should be regarded as a symptom of these inner confusions. Only by looking to the causes of the illegible, super-rigid script, can any improvements be expected. As levels of anxiety and aggression decline it will prove far easier to help the child relax his writing and so produce, within a still unique style, a script which is easy to read.

The important lessons to be learned from this example of writing can be summarised as follows:

1. Rigid angles and an absence of curved strokes indicate anxiety, tenseness and actually aggressive or latently aggressive behaviour expressed as stubbornness, passive resistance or a refusal to conform to adult expectations.

2. Unnecessary overwriting, such as the heavy full-stops and double circle letters 'O' in the above example, are characteristic of anxious striving and sensitivity to criticism.

3. Mistakes which have been heavily crossed out, the pen going over the error again and again, are signs that the writer has a higher than normal feeling of anxiety about making mistakes

and experiences frustration over his, or her, imagined incompetence.

Co-ordination Problems

The handwriting shown in the sample here is also difficult to read, but differs markedly in the form of illegibility shown in the first example.

Fig. 2.

There are four major differences to be noted.

1. It is not super-rigid, but over-released. Proper direction and adequate forcefulness of the handwriting movement has, therefore, proved highly difficult.
2. The first sample is over-controlled, this is under-controlled.
3. While the first lacked fluency this lacks co-ordination.
4. The first is tight with an overly firm stroke, this is flabby and has wavering strokes.

In the second example a lack of control in the handwriting reveals itself in an inability to direct the movements of pen on paper. The strokes waver and are jerky, with the writer apparently at the mercy of sudden, random directional impulses which can be seen throughout the script.

This poor control over the handwriting is often accompanied by a lack of behavioural control, resulting in impulsive behaviour in other areas of life. The writer often tends to act first and consider the consequences later.

This writing by a fourteen-year-old girl shows marked impulsivity combined with a lack of co-ordination. Such writers tend to appear clumsy and sometimes accident-prone. They are easily distracted and find it hard to concentrate on a single topic for any length of time. They may move quickly from one pursuit to another, hardly bothering to get into a pursuit before dropping it for something different. These tendencies are usually found in adolescents who show this type of 'uncontrolled' legibility.

In order to help this type of writer improve the legibility of their script it is again essential to take into account their personality, and how they respond to all aspects of life.

These two examples show poor handwriting caused by completely different difficulties in the lives of their young writers. The first is over-controlled, the second suffers from a lack of control. These factors are the keys to the two contrasting personalities. Yet both children are about the same age and attend the same school, they are matched in social class, background and in the amount of teaching received. These similarities help to underline the individuality of handwriting, as an expression of inner needs, at all ages. Since personality and activity levels play such a crucial role in the growth of the child, such an analysis provides the background to an understanding of mental and physical development.

HANDWRITING AND GROWTH

As with most of the skills acquired by children during the process of growing up, handwriting is a dynamic ability which develops throughout education. Just as some children surge ahead, and others fall behind, in the growth of originality, imagination, creativity, logical reasoning and other mental attributes, so does the rate at which handwriting matures vary considerably from one child to the next. Since its increasing sophistication mirrors the successful growth of intellectual skills in other areas, handwriting can be used as a gauge by which to judge the child's rate of mental development.

When writing is being learned, the child strives to make as close a copy as possible of the model supplied by the teacher.

With practice, however, handwriting grows increasingly automatic or *overlearned* and becomes a means of expressing ideas rather than a skill in its own right. As this starts to happen, the child may develop an originality of style which departs from the school model or there may be a continued, rigid adherence to the copybook letter forms. By monitoring these changes and noting the age at which an individual style appears it is possible to detect a wide range of developmental changes. We can assess the rate of mental growth, discover originality of expression and begin to learn something of the possible difficulties which the child is facing.

Early and Late Developers

Compare the two samples of handwriting below.

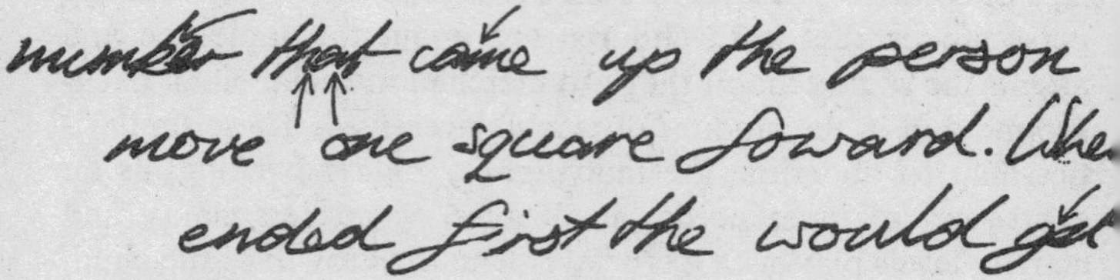

Fig. 3.
Original Style

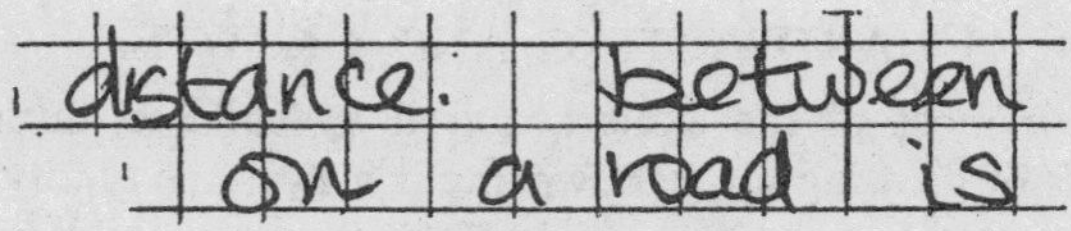

Fig. 4.
Copybook Style

Both were produced by ten-year-old children although it is hard to appreciate this fact from the very different scripts. The first has an adult's style with considerable departures from the school-taught form and many original features which are quite remarkable in a child of that age. The second example deviates very little from the copybook, shows little originality, but is about average for a ten-year-old.

The sophisticated script of the first child tells us a number of important things about the writer.

He is likely to be more independent and self-sufficient than other children of his age and will, almost certainly, have developed his own way of doing things in other activities as well. Our research has shown that children with this degree of originality are likely to be ahead of their companions in several areas of development, and to be more mature than children of the same age. This greater maturity may not always be apparent to other adults, however, and particularly to their teachers. Because such children are intellectually advanced, they may get bored easily and become frustrated at the constant repetition of tasks which have been mastered quickly and easily. While the other pupils are still struggling to grasp some concept or solve a problem, they are often waiting with growing impatience for further intellectual stimulation. The boredom they experience as a result can lead to disruptive behaviour or a withdrawal of attention. Because of this, their school work sometimes appears worse than that of less able pupils. They may even receive lower marks, poorer grades and gain a reputation as trouble-makers. These adult perceptions can lead to the child re-evaluating his, or her, own abilities and losing self-confidence as a result. This loss of confidence can produce a variety of responses, depending on the personality of the child, ranging from anxiety to aggression.

Children who are troublesome in class, or who seem to have fallen behind after an early promise of brightness, may well be victims of this all too frequent syndrome. Their handwriting can be used to check accelerated mental development which may lie behind these difficulties.

Such children often appear isolated from companions of the same age because they prefer the company of adults or older children. This should be encouraged as it is through contact with more mature minds that the early developer finds much needed stimulation. The same can be said about hobbies or pursuits which may strike some adults as being 'too advanced for the child's age'. Rather than discourage such activities, however, the perceptive parent will offer help and advice. An out-of-school pursuit which absorbs and excites a bright child can help to compensate for any lack of stimulation in the classroom.

It is useful to look out for signs of high levels of anxiety in the early developer – the example of original style above has such indications in the sudden narrowing of certain words (indicated by arrows). Such anxiety arises, in many instances, because the child becomes confused about the way he is expected to behave at school or at home.

The above average child is, by definition, set apart from his, or her, companions and few people enjoy the feeling of being different. Sometimes a bright child will deliberately fail so as not to outshine school friends, brothers or sisters.

It is essential, when offering praise to this type of child, not to use their abilities as a stick with which to beat the less capable. The kind of remarks often heard in schools and homes which contrast the attainments of children – 'Why can't you be as clever as Simon?' – are damaging to all concerned, not least the child being used as a shining intellectual example to others. Research by one of the present authors (David Lewis) has shown that this type of double-edged praise is very likely to diminish the performance of the bright child while doing nothing to improve achievement levels in the more average youngster.

Children whose handwriting lacks originality and sophistication are less likely to be early developers. They may, however, give the appearance of being above average intellectually and do well in school subjects. In some instances this is achieved by excessively hard work rather than a superior intelligence. While the early developer may deliberately reduce performance in order to appear more average, the average developer who wants to stay ahead often works constantly at the limits of their mental abilities so as to keep up with the leaders. Where the handwriting of such children shows indications of frustration stress, or anxiety, it may be warning of difficulties ahead.

Children who strive harder than most for achievement are under considerable intellectual strain. At times of special pressure – for example during examinations – this additional stress may lead to emotional disturbances. The child may become very irritable, or moody, subject to tantrums or outbursts of crying, loss of appetite or disturbed sleep. In extreme cases there may be psychosomatic illness.

This is most likely to happen when the need for a high level of achievement results from adult pressures. The vast majority of children crave affection and praise from grown-ups, especially their parents. In order to win and hold a love which is conditional or appears to them to be conditional on school success, children often drive themselves to the point of breakdown. This dependency provides ambitious mothers and fathers with a powerful means of pressurising children into fulfilling their own dreams and desires. For instance, the father who was forced to leave school early may have a strong wish for his son or daughter to shine academically and go on to higher education. Deliberately, or without being aware of the fact, this desire locks the child into an educational pressure cooker. They have to achieve high grades, top marks, excellent reports in order to satisfy their father's dream. Any failure is seen in terms of letting down somebody whom they love and whose love they need. Very often such failures are, in fact, punished by a withdrawal of affection by the adults. There can be few more anxiety-producing situations for any child than this combination of excessively hard work and guilt-inducing penalties.

If a situation arises where a highly achieving child, whose handwriting indicates only an average level of development begins to show signs of anxiety or emotional disturbance, the discrepancy between intellectual ability and academic success should be considered a possible underlying cause. If you are that child's parent then try to reassess your attitudes towards school achievement. If you are the child's teacher then consider how he, or she, can best be helped. Perhaps a discussion with the parents will produce a more reasonable attitude. Failing that it may be possible to ease the burden at school so that the same level of achievement is maintained with slightly less effort.

The development of an original handwriting style is often slowed down by the attitudes of adults towards what constitutes 'good' writing. We mentioned earlier, in connection with legibility, that content should be examined as objectively as possible without its merits – or otherwise – being coloured by the neatness of the writing. A strict insistence on a child following the copybook form can lead to a retardation of handwriting development, a suppression of creativity and a decline of interest in expressing ideas creatively. Instead of concentrating on the thoughts and original concepts which they would like to express, the child burdened down with a need to follow a strict handwriting style focuses attention on script formation rather than content.

Handwriting is a highly personal expression of many physical and psychological forces, in children just as much as in adults. The young have every right to develop their own writing style and, so long as it is legible, should be encouraged to do so. Teachers and parents must avoid a strait-jacket approach which places a greater value on presentation than creativity and delays – perhaps permanently – the growth of a sophisticated, personalised handwriting.

HANDWRITING ORIGINALITY GUIDE

To assess the level of originality in a sample of children's handwriting, compare the script to the examples below. These cover normal and above average styles in three age groups from seven to twelve years. Beyond this age it is much harder to detect early development through handwriting variations since most children will, by this time, have achieved a non-copybook style.

Age Range 7–8 years
Normal Development

Fig. 5.

Above Average Development

I Just cant

underseand it.

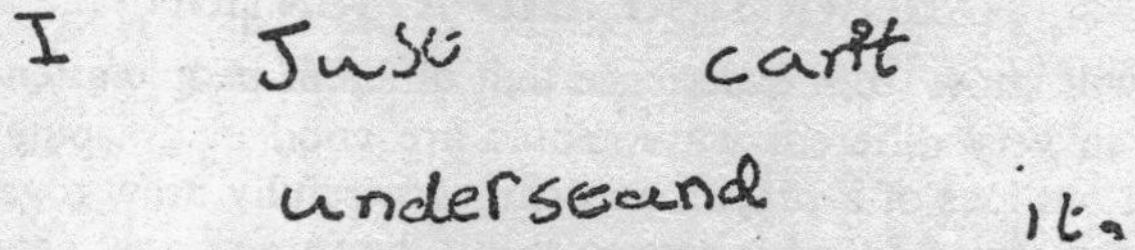

Fig. 6.

Age Range 9–10 years
Normal Development

June I went on holiday to
I went to see some

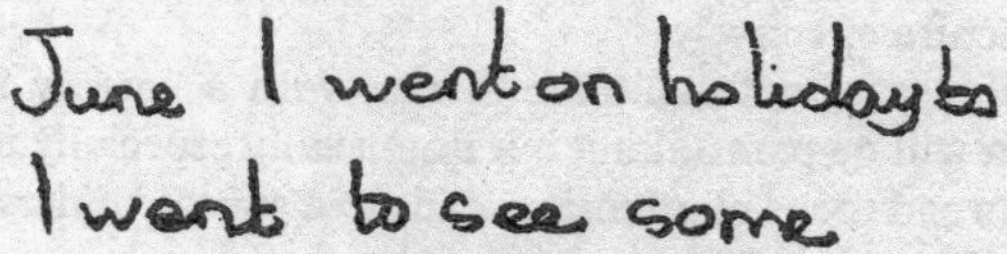

Fig. 7.

Above Average Development

Liqur is something as high

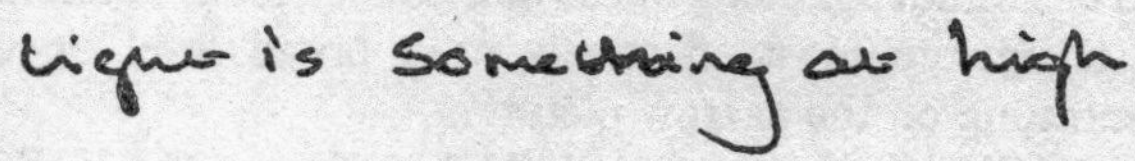

Fig. 8.

Age Range 11–12+ years
Normal Development

ruined by all
and reduced to
was wise and

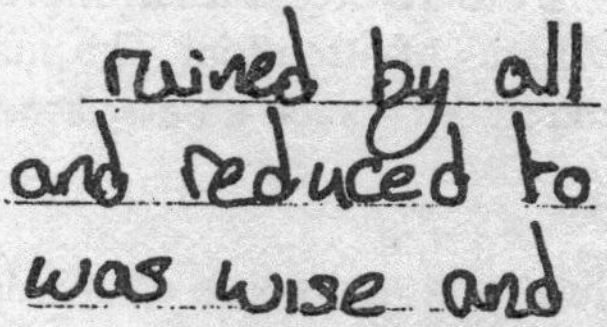

Fig. 9.

Above Average Development

what a lovely summer's day!

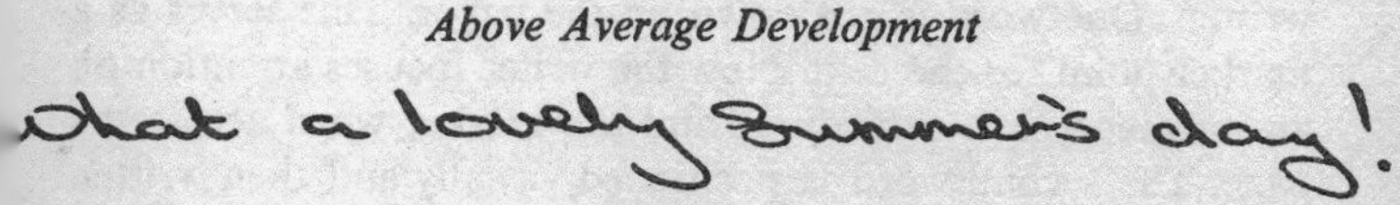

Fig. 10.

HANDWRITING AND ATTENTION

You will know from experience that different people attend to tasks in very different ways. Some are good at grasping the broad outlines of a project and can successfully draw together a wide range of different concepts. But they are poor at detailed planning, making slapdash mistakes and foolish errors. Others are first class when it comes to fine details and will take meticulous care over drawing up complex schemes. Yet their focus of attention is too narrow for them to be able to see the wider picture effectively.

It is the same with children. Those with a narrow focus of attention will be painstaking but not usually especially inspired, while a broad focus of attention leads to a superb understanding of overall concepts but a poor execution of details.

In order to bring about the best performance from both types of child – and indeed both kinds of adult – it is necessary to have a clear understanding of the individual's focus of attention. Does it operate most effectively at a broad level or when concentrating on the narrow picture?

Handwriting, because it is a skill which demands a high level of narrow-focused attention, provides the most reliable guide to these different mental approaches. It is especially helpful with young children because their handwriting has not yet become over-learned. It is, therefore, rather more likely to reflect differences in the focus-of-attention. The main indications to watch out for when making such an assessment are as follows:

Straightness of Line

In order to produce a straight line of words the writer must combine a high level of visual feedback with a fine focus-of-attention. Consider the sequence of movements as a line is written. One word is put down on the paper. This serves as a marker point for the next. Now the writer focuses attention on an imaginary line extending from the marker word across the page. The second word is positioned visually and then written down. Each word that follows either confirms the accuracy of the line or shows up defects in evenness. At each stage the eye must send very precise information to the brain and coordinate the placing of the word through fine adjustments to the writing muscles. It is a task of considerable complexity which makes great demands on attention.

With practice, achieving a straight line on plain paper becomes a fairly routine task. But it is no simple matter for young children. Not only do they lack the necessary practice but their span of attention is poorly developed. It is hard for them to focus for long on small details and the line may drift wildly; as a result line straightness may be used to provide an index of developing focus-of-attention and improved mental abilities.

You can assess line straightness in a sample of handwriting by matching it to the examples in the chart below. As a general rule you should remember that lines which are evenly spaced and parallel show an effective focus-of-attention, while unevenly spaced and wavy lines are an indication that visual feedback is poor and the focus-of-attention inadequate.

Line Straightness Chart

To assess an handwriting sample simply refer to the appropriate age group and match the writing to the most appropriate three categories.

Line Straightness Chart

Ages 7–9
Category One
Good Alignment

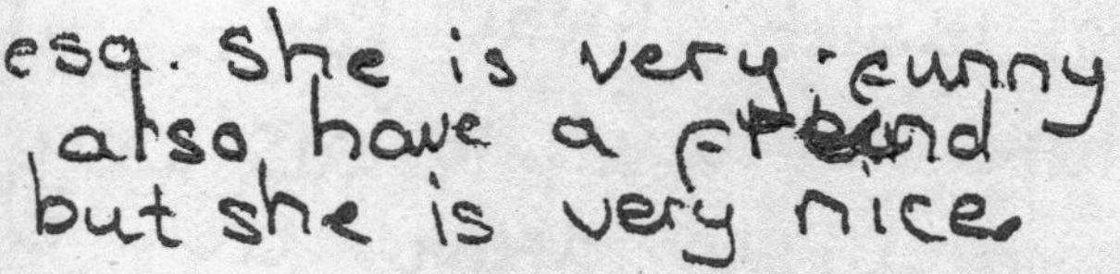

esq. she is very funny
also have a friend
but she is very nice.

Fig. 11.

Category Two
Normal Alignment

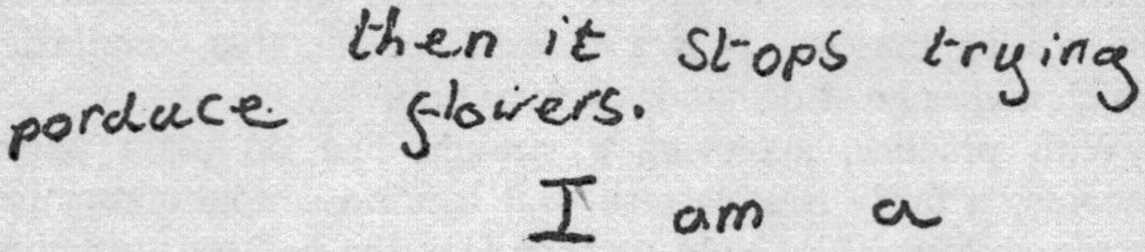

pordace
then it stops trying
flowers.
I am a

Fig. 12.

Category Three
Poor Alignment

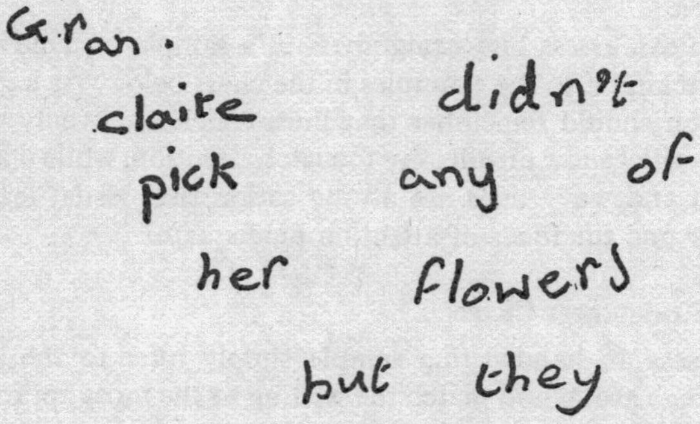

Gran.
claire   didn't
pick   any   of
her   flowers
but   they

Fig. 13.

Ages 10–11
Category One
Good Alignment

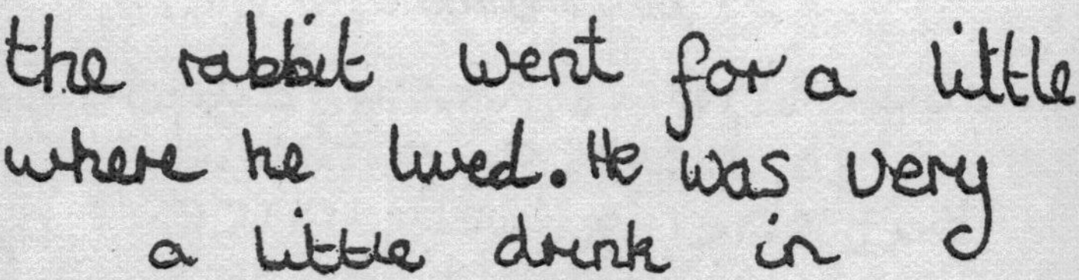

the rabbit went for a little
where he lived. He was very
a little drink in

Fig. 14.

Category Two
Normal Alignment

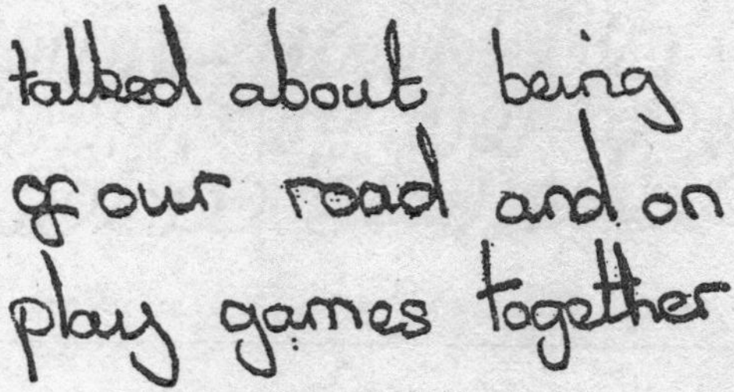

talked about being
of our road and on
play games together

Fig. 15.

Category Three
Poor Alignment

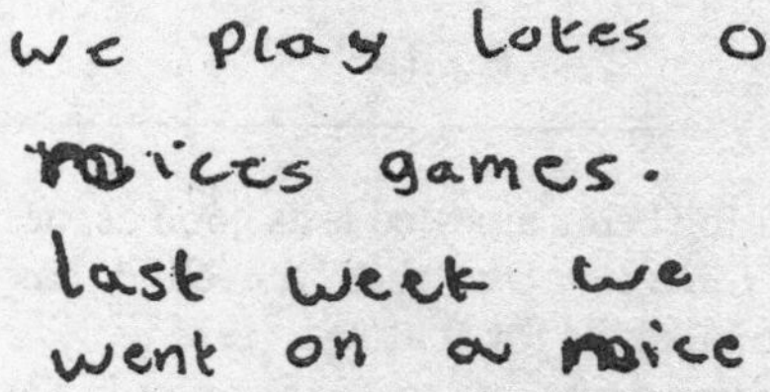

we play lotes og.

roices games.
last week we
went on a noice

Fig. 16.

Age 12+
Category One
Good Alignment

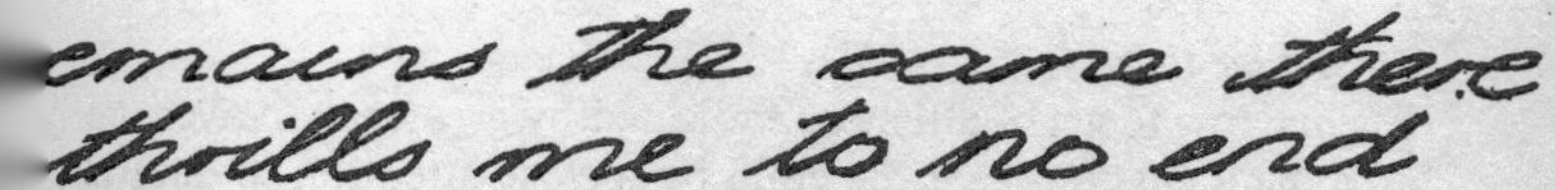

emains the came there
thrills me to no end

Fig. 17.

Category Two
Normal Alignment

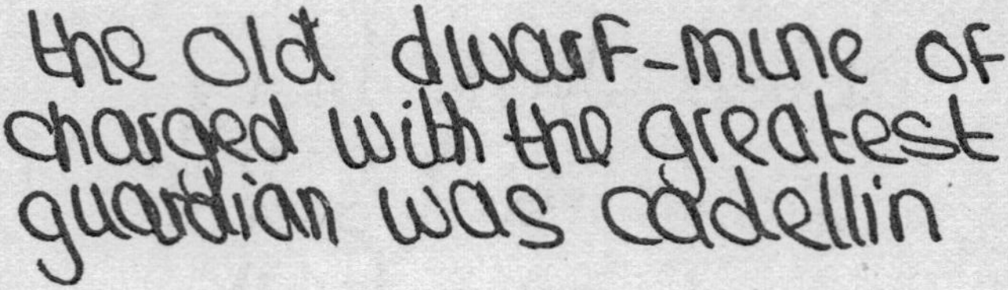

the old dwarf-mine of
charged with the greatest
guardian was cadellin

Fig. 18.

Category Three
Poor Alignment

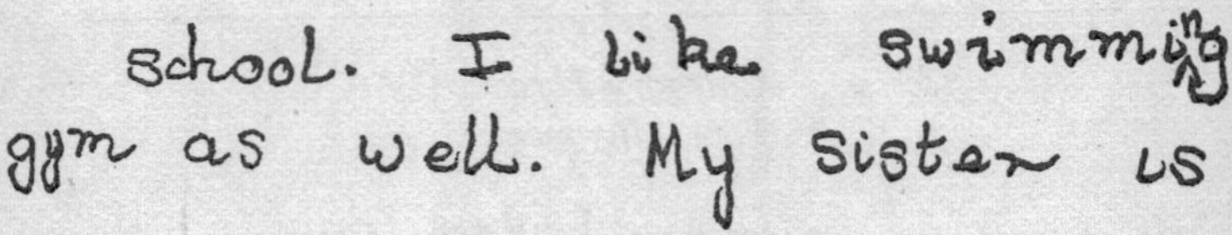

school. I like swimming
gym as well. My sister is

Fig. 19.

If the handwriting being assessed is as good as, or better than, that shown in *Category One* then the child has developed superior attentional skills for that age.

If the handwriting compares to the samples in *Category Two* it indicates average attentional skills.

Handwriting which is as poor as, or worse than, that shown in *Category Three* indicates a below average development of attentional skills.

What Line Straightness Tells You

Straighter than Average Lines
The narrow focus of attention indicated by greater than average alignment suggests that the child pays close attention to details but may miss the wider issues involved in a task. It is associated with independence, self-reliance and the need to work things out for themselves. Such children will trust their own judge-

ments and may not be emotionally forthcoming as they prefer to keep inner feelings to themselves.

Better than average line straightness is characteristic of a child with considerable analytical ability who enjoys practical, scientific or technical challenges. Any course of action will be considered from all angles before being adopted and they seldom do anything on impulse. This type of child can appear very stubborn at times because they insist on finding things out for themselves and pay close attention to the smallest points.

Because they prefer logical approach to most things, the most effective form of persuasion is rational argument rather than emotional appeals, threats or coercion. To enable the considerable potential of these children to be realised, their special way of looking at life must be understood and respected. Allow them to make their own decisions in their own time. They will probably be happiest when working on practical problems, but should be encouraged to see both the wider picture as well as the essential details.

Worse than Average Line Straightness

These children have a wide focus-of-attention, see problems as a whole and tend to overlook finer details. They are usually impulsive and rely on intuition rather than logic or a careful analysis of the situation.

Because a narrow focus-of-attention is needed for success in many school subjects, this type of child may not shine in academic subjects. They are more likely to excel in tasks which offer the maximum scope for their imagination and skill at grasping overall concepts. They will probably dislike science and technical subjects and do best in areas which do not demand a purely analytical or logical approach – languages, arts or social studies. Children with a wide focus-of-attention tend to need others around them and work best in company rather than in the isolation preferred by the narrow focus child. Their manual dexterity is poorer than average and they are more likely to fail at tasks requiring great co-ordination.

Letter Reversal

A sign sometimes seen in the handwriting of children with special problems of attention is the reversed letter, where for example a 'b' is written in mistake for a 'd' or a 'p' for a 'q'.

Studies by Dr. L. J. Chapman, an American educational researcher, have shown that where letter reversal is a persistent feature in their writing, children have a very poor focus-of-attention. Where reversed letters occur the comments made above apply even more strongly. Reversed letters which are found in the script of children who have been writing for more than two years diagnose an attentional disability which should be overcome with the help of a remedial teacher.

Anxiety and Handwriting

Children's writing can provide a clear guide to many types of anxiety problem, difficulties which you might not be able to notice so readily, or so early, through other means. We have already discussed some of the anxiety indications in previous chapters, and you will find a complete list of them in our directory of the hidden language in the last chapter. Here we want to describe one sign which is almost exclusively found in the handwriting of the very young. Where it occurs you can diagnose several types of anxiety, insecurity and fear response.

Columning

In the handwriting sample below, a fearful nine-year-old boy has carefully arranged his words in stacks, each one having been placed directly beneath the word on the line above rather than allowed to flow naturally across the page.

When viewed from a normal reading distance the stacked letters give the appearance of having white 'columns' between them. This is a small, compulsive gesture which reveals an over-concern with order arising from the child's above average feelings of anxiety and insecurity. Young writers who develop this style are usually fearful of authority, although they will

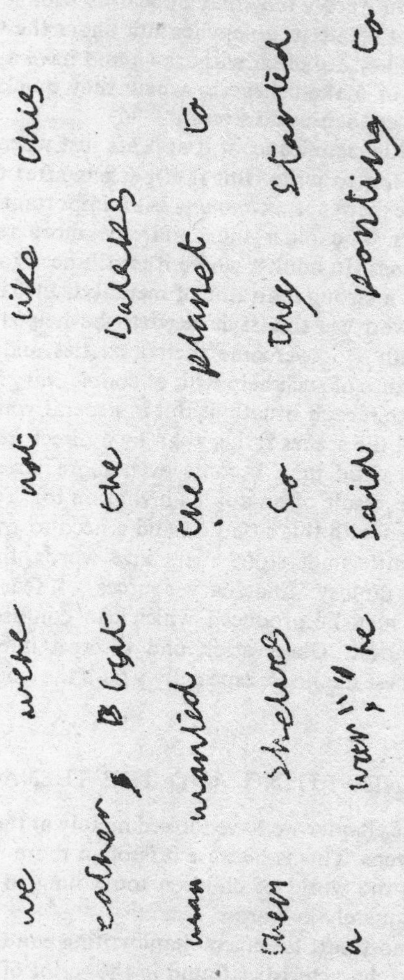

Fig. 20.

often try to defy adults in ways unlikely to attract attention and retribution. Outwardly they may appear exceedingly polite and compliant, but create trouble when not under the watchful eye of an adult. They are often withdrawn and have a rich fantasy life, a world of make-believe to which they quickly retreat at times of greater than usual stress.

This has little significance if it appears just when the child is starting to learn to write. But if it persists after two years of handwriting experience, *columning* is an important indicator of inner feelings. The older the child, the more revealing this feature becomes. In adults, where it is still occasionally found, columning is a strong indicator of mental disturbance.

Children who use this style need to be helped, gently and sympathetically, to overcome their anxieties and insecurities. The exact nature of such help will, of course, vary from child to child and within each situation. But in general you should seek to act behind the scenes rather than by a direct frontal assault. The anxious child may become even more stressed and insecure as the result of an adult's invitation to: 'Tell me what's wrong.' Faced with this situation and a need to translate their, frequently, little understood fears into words, the child may retreat into fantasy. Imaginary sources of fear and causes for distress may be produced which can confuse the would-be helpful adult. Observation and discreet intervention are usually the best methods, especially where the younger child is concerned.

HANDWRITING AND THE TEENAGER

So far in this chapter we have looked mainly at the handwriting of the pre-teens. This is because it is often more useful to have insight into the world of children too young to express their feelings adequately in words.

For the most part teenagers' handwriting can be assessed on many of the characteristics found in the script of adults. However, there are some indications which have a particular relevance to this period of life. An analysis of the writing of teenagers can help concerned adults towards a fuller appreciation of the traumas that frequently accompany the difficult transition from adolescence to adulthood. As this change takes place the structure of the young person's relationships change and dependency on parents declines. It would be remarkable if the dramatic, emotional upheavals which accompany a search for independence and identity were not, in some way, reflected in handwriting. Research has shown that this is indeed what happens. The script of teenagers reveals clear patterns and signs.

One of the most consistent changes is a sudden decrease in handwriting pressure which occurs towards the mid-teenage years. First identified by Clare Roman at New York's Handwriting Institute it has since been observed in the writing of almost every adolescent examined. Decreased pressure usually persists for a period of two years, after which it returns to the previous level. As we explained in chapter three, such a decrease often forms part of the writer's 'flight response' from a stressful situation. The frequency with which it occurs in the handwriting of fifteen- to seventeen-year-olds shows that, although they may give little outward expression of distress, the majority of youngsters find adolescence a stressful period of life from which they desire to escape.

It is a wise precaution to keep a special check on handwriting pressure during the mid-teens, especially if there are any more obvious signs of emotional difficulties. Parents and teachers will thus be able to identify the onset of this period and help the child accordingly. But such monitoring should only occur with the knowledge and consent of the young person concerned. Such a respect for their right of privacy is essential if good relations are to be maintained.

The handwriting of teenagers often shows specific examples of style in addition to the widely-found pressure changes. These modifications of the script can be interpreted as a strong desire on the part of the writer to develop a distinct and separate identity.

Around the middle-teens, many writers adopt a marked backward slant to their script. This was associated with emotional disturbance in chapter seven when we discussed backward slant in adult handwriting. When used by teenagers, however, it is much more likely to indicate an expression of individuality and should be seen as evidence that the writer is striving for a less dependent, more adult lifestyle. A backward slant is thought to make the writing appear more original and interesting. It normally reverts back to a more conventional angle within a couple of years.

Decoration of the letters, convoluted signatures, flourishing underlining of names and similar distinctive but unnecessary signs serve the same purpose. They aim to transform the mundane task of writing into forms of self expression in an obvious and dramatic manner. One of these decorative touches is the circular 'i' dot described in chapter six. As with backward slant this needs to be interpreted differently when seen in the handwriting of adolescents, and regarded as an eye-catching embellishment rather than a desire to appear socially sophisticated. The same applies to the use of extra loops on the lower strokes of letters such as 'p', 'q' and 'y'.

Highly decorated capital letters may be used and where these are original and harmonious they reveal a well developed aesthetic sense as illustrated in the example below.

Fig. 21.

Research into the analysis of children's handwriting continues. Our own long-term study includes an investigation of the relationship between certain aspects of the child's body language and both writing and drawing abilities. In time it will certainly be possible to discover even more information on the basis of such observations.

Already, as we have tried to show in this chapter, there is much to be learned from the interpretation of children's handwriting at all ages. It should not be seen as a substitute for more conventional approaches to understanding, of course. But accurate analysis will provide both confirmation of assessments made by other means and offer new avenues of exploration to all those concerned with obtaining a more thorough insight into the minds of the very young.

Chapter Ten

The Hidden Language of Handwriting

As you will now realise the analysis of handwriting is rather like painting a picture. Each pen stroke, like every movement of the brush, must be considered carefully. But, while concentrating on the finer details, it is essential never to lose sight of the overall scene!

Interpreting a person's script should be seen as a dynamic process which demands that the analyst bring together a whole series of characteristics present in individual letters, in the shape of words and in the flow and direction of whole lines. It is not merely a matter of isolating and identifying specific signs within the writing, but of drawing a number of indications and conclusions together to present a rounded image of the writer. Everything present in the script, from the colour of the ink and the straightness of the writing lines to the pressure used and the style of strokes, has to be considered both on its own and as part of the overall story which the handwriting has to tell. Only by this sort of holistic approach can an accurate conclusion be arrived at and the most helpful, reliable and informative predictions be made.

Handwriting is an expression of personality, health, emotional state, intellectual ability and activity level. One aspect of the script may enhance and emphasise another portion or oppose and contradict it. In order to be valid and useful your analysis must take these interacting forces into account. Here is what might happen during an interpretation. You have a sample which contains very heavy pressure – indicating a high level of activity – but also shows signs of physical weakness (see chapter eight). It would not be very constructive simply to comment that: 'The writer is very active but experiences physical weakness.' While both statements would be correct their interpretation is far from satisfactory.

A more useful assessment, which makes use of these – and other – indications in the writing might read as follows: 'The writer has an inherently high level of activity. However, physical weakness appears to be such that it limits his abundant supplies of energy. This may be expected to cause a degree of frustration since he is accustomed to expending a great deal of effort in everyday pursuits. He is likely to push himself too hard in order to compensate for this apparent lack of energy and may put his health at risk as a result.'

An analysis along these lines not only combines and gives the correct weight to the two indications, but performs the useful service of warning the writer of a possible health threat due to trying too hard during a period of physical weakness.

This example is far less subtle than a full analysis, based on a consideration of the whole multitude of handwriting signs would normally allow. In order to achieve the most accurate and penetrating interpretation, therefore, it is essential to pay close attention to *all* aspects of the handwriting being analysed and, more importantly, to have developed an understanding of human functioning as the sum total of its emotional, personality, physical and motivational components. This understanding is not a skill which can be acquired from any book, but must be developed through constant and perceptive observation of one's fellow human beings. The cost demanded for such a uniquely important education is an investment of time on your part far greater than that needed to master the basic procedures of graphonomy – but you will find the effort well rewarded.

PRACTICAL CONSIDERATIONS

Before starting an analysis you should try to discover the age and sex of the writer. Although the actual writing signs are the same for either sex and at most ages, the advice you offer on the basis of your interpretation will clearly be very different.

If the handwriting reveals indications of serious emotional

disturbance or illness, either mental or physical, you must consider very carefully how this information should be given to the writer. It may, indeed, be preferable to keep the knowledge to yourself, unless there is some positive way in which the writer can be helped. When you do decide to give unpleasant news to anybody do so in the most tactful and diplomatic manner possible. Bear in mind the cautions which we have expressed about the fallibility of *all* forms of assessment and remember that handwriting does not give any sort of diagnosis where serious illness is concerned. It can only indicate risk and warn.

Always maintain the highest standards of confidentiality about the handwriting you analyse and the conclusions you draw. Never discuss the interpretation with anybody else unless you have the writer's express permission. This need for confidentiality extends even to close relatives and friends on those occasions when you are specifically asked not to mention the assessment.

As we mentioned in chapter one, and have tried to stress throughout the book, graphonomy is not to be taken lightly or used irresponsibly. Its procedures are deep and penetrating. They reveal information about the writer in clear terms rather than vague generalisations. Treat them seriously and with respect. If you are not certain of your conclusions, or hesitant about how to express them tactfully, then it is much better to say nothing. At first you will certainly be eager to analyse all the samples of handwriting which come your way. There is nothing wrong with this, provided you bear in mind our advice about the need for caution and discretion. But, as you become more experienced, you will find that it is far better to wait for people to ask you for an analysis – and to make certain they *really* want to discover as much about themselves as graphonomy can tell them – before agreeing to carry out an analysis or make an assessment.

PUTTING YOUR KNOWLEDGE INTO PRACTICE

The only way to learn graphonomy is to carry out practical

interpretations of handwriting samples. In order to help you gain some basic experience, without running any risk of making embarrassing mistakes in public, this chapter contains two samples of handwriting which we have analysed in detail. After the first example, our report is set out in full. We have included all the relevant characteristics found within the script and described at length what these mean.

If you would like to try your hand at an analysis before reading our first report then by all means do so. On the other hand, if you would prefer to read the completed assessment to see what a full analysis should look like, a second example has also been included. We suggest that you attempt an interpretation of this sample before reading our report in order to see how your report compares with ours.

To help you with the analysis more than sixty of the most important handwriting signs discussed in the book have been collected together in a dictionary of the hidden language which follows this chapter.

When analysing the second sample you will probably find it helpful to refer to both the Directory and the previous report in order to identify most of the major signs present in the handwriting and relate them together in such a way

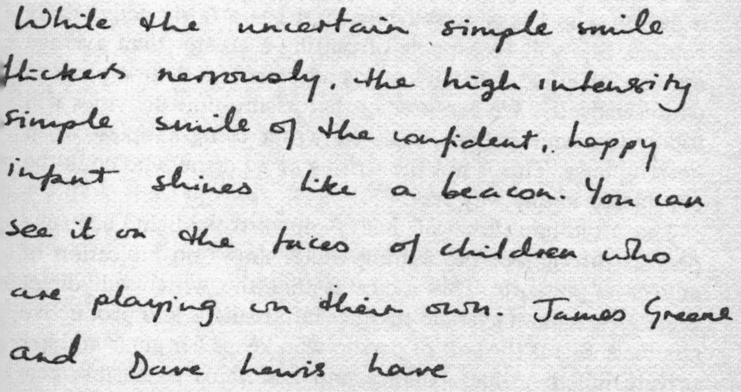

While the uncertain simple smile flickers nervously, the high intensity simple smile of the confident, happy infant shines like a beacon. You can see it on the faces of children who are playing on their own. James Greene and Dave Lewis have

Fig. 1.

that a dynamic, three-dimensional portrait of the writer is created.

Example One

The handwriting above was produced by a female student, aged 22. She is an attractive girl, unmarried but with a steady boyfriend. Usually amusing and outward-going she can occasionally be moody and depressed. She is a highly-strung girl who finds her studies, especially examinations, something of an ordeal. At the time the sample was produced she was going through a difficult emotional period. We should add that the above information was obtained only *after* an analysis of her handwriting had been made. It was not known at the time this interpretation was produced.

The Analysis

Using the Funnel System of analysis we start by taking into account the overall aspects of the writing, that is *pressure and flow*.

The script pressure varies considerably but appears to be slightly heavier than average. This indicates a somewhat higher than usual level of activity. The writer is, therefore, likely to be a person who keeps herself busy and has a fairly active daily routine. She will be capable of putting a greater than average amount of effort into any task and starts most new projects enthusiastically. We can predict that leisure-time activities will follow the same pattern, with the writer being happiest when keeping busy. This is not the writing of a person who could be considered in any way lazy.

The rhythmic flow of heavy downstroke/light upstroke persists throughout the writing which shows no indication of any cross-pressure. This indicates that the writer will direct these greater than average energies into realistic and productive channels. She is the sort of person who keeps her goals and her private life in proper balance and maintains a sensible perspective on the relative merits of each. She is unlikely to be tempted to sacrifice valued relationships for the sake of material success.

The handwriting shows considerable random variability of pressure throughout the sample. Notice, for example, the word 'confident' in line three. Compare the pressure in the letters 'o' and 'n' to the downstroke pressure in the letter 'f' of the same word. Similar pressure contrast is evident elsewhere in the script, a trend which is accompanied by sudden pressure *increases* for example in the 'k' of 'like' (line four) and elsewhere in the script. This indicates that the writer is unstable and will probably fly off the handle too easily. She is probably nervous, quick-tempered and has a sensitive temperament.

The writing is more released than rigid, but still not as released as the examples shown in chapter four. This indicates that she prefers the novel to the familiar and variety to routine. She expresses her emotions readily and the released writing combined with irregular pressure suggests that these fluctuate widely between elation and despondency.

The handwriting is considerably simplified which places her close to Category Three of general intelligence (chapter four), that is on the same level of IQ as demanded by such professions as teachers, computer programmers and journalists. Notice the simplified 'g' used throughout the script. As we have already explained, research has shown this letter formation to indicate an above average level of education.

All the 'i' dots are carefully formed with the dot close to the stem stroke of the letter in many cases, so the writer cannot be considered a detached and self-sufficient individual of the type described in chapter six.

The capitals are approximately the same size as the upper strokes of ascenders. This shows that the writer strikes a balance between being too assertive or too submissive. She will not attempt to dominate others, neither will she be prepared to allow them to treat her unfairly. This gives her a score of zero on the Assertiveness Scale and, since the capitals are *not* smaller than the ascending strokes, zero on the Submissiveness Scale as well.

The writing is rather small and has falling lines. These trends are not marked, however, and the writer scores two on the Perfectionism Scale. This tells us that Perfectionism (see chapter six) is only a mild trend in her personality, although one which must be taken into account when producing the final assessment. She will be more orderly and methodical than most, and tend to be fussier in many situations than the circumstances warrant. She prefers to take a logical approach to problems rather than acting on intuition.

The lack of downward 't' cross-strokes in the sample suggest that the writer may not have a great need for achievement or overly high ambitions.

The sudden, sharp increases in pressure give the writer a score of two points on the Aggression Scale, suggesting that she is prone to argument, can be stubborn and may show other signs of aggression. These are not marked trends, however, and will not be a dominant feature of her personality.

The slight rightward slant and rightward extension of the small of the script gives her a score of 3 on the Extraversion Scale. The lengths of the lower strokes on descenders (i.e. 'j'; 'g'; 'y') and the width of the small letters are not great enough to add any more points on this trait. A score of Three on the Extraversion Scale is near average and the writer will show only a small amount of the behaviour associated with extraversion. This means she is mildly sociable, outgoing and gregarious, and will show a normal amount of impulsivity, sensation-seeking and risk-taking.

As the writer does not use circular 'i' dots or decorated lower loops she scores zero on the Sophistication Scale. In fact, since the lower loops are simplified and austere, she is not likely to put on an act or worldliness or social pretensions and will be more sincere in expression of feelings towards others than those whose script contains these embellishments.

Although there is still a great deal of information to be extracted from the handwriting, which will have to be included in our final assessment, it is possible – at this point – to construct a Personality Profile as described in chapter six.

Personality Profile

Trait	None	Mild	Moderate	Sub-stantial	Extreme
	0	1–3	4–5	6–8	9–10
Independence	0	0	0	0	0
Assertive	0	0	0	0	0
Submissive	0	0	0	0	0
Perfectionism	0	0	0	0	0
Ambition	0	0	0	0	0
Aggression	0	0	0	0	0
Extraversion	0	0	0	0	0
Sophistication	0	0	0	0	0

What conclusions can be drawn from this handwriting? So far as the eight major personality traits are concerned the girl shows a perfectly normal Profile. That is, we would not expect her to behave in a way likely to surprise other people, or lead them to conclude she was in any way odd or eccentric.

However the script does contain clear signs of *emotional disturbance*.

Notice first of all the variability in size of the small letters. For example, in the words 'flickers nervously' (line two) the 's' in 'flickers' is twice the height of the 'e' and 'r'. The letters 'e', 'r' and 'v' in 'nervous' in this line are all of different heights. This variability is a dominant trend throughout the sample.

A second sign associated with emotional problems, also present in this writer's script, is the narrowing of the upper loops in the ascenders, in most cases even to the point where the upstroke of the loop overlaps the downstroke. Look, for example, at the construction of the letter 'l' in the word 'simple' (line one).

Finally, we have the slightly greater than normal waviness of the writing lines and the erratic pressure, with sudden sharp increases in pressure. These add weight to our interpretation that this handwriting has been produced by somebody with moderate emotional disturbance. The writer is nervous, excitable, and probably experiences greater than average feelings of guilt. Her emotions are liable to colour her judgements and to intrude unnecessarily into personal relationships. That is, she will tend to become emotional in situations where such a response is not called for and may even prove detrimental to happiness. She worries excessively and may sleep badly at times. There will be occasional lapses of concentration.

No signs of emotional constraint or compulsiveness (see chapter seven) can be detected in the script. This suggests that she gives vent to her emotions and does not keep them bottled up or try to defend herself against them by means of repetitive actions.

Several indications of stress (see chapter eight) can be found in the handwriting. There are clear signs of *fading* in the word 'confident' (line three) which starts with a loss of pressure in the upper part of the letter 'c', where the writer began the initial stroke of the letter, and extends as far as the letter 'o'. The considerable length of this fading means that the indication must be taken seriously. This sympton of stress is confirmed by the presence of resting dots in the script, for instance in the 'w' of 'while' (line one) where the dot appears at the end of the last upward movement of the letter. There are also a few examples of sudden waviness, for example in the 'i' of 'flickers' (line two) and the first 'n' in 'confident' (line three), and broken strokes in the 'e' of 'uncertain' – and in the 's' of 'Lewis' (lines one and seven).

These signs show that the writer is under considerable stress and is experiencing physical strain as a result. She is probably overtired and tense as the result of some specific and stressful situation. There are no signs of mental or physical illness.

Our analysis suggests that the writer's degree of emotional disturbance may have arisen as the result of a temporary condition and not be a permanent feature of her personality. In any event the present state of affairs increases the likelihood of emotional outbursts, a tendency which seems to be a more lasting aspect of her emotional make-up. She flairs up rapidly in response to stressful events and is quick to show hostility. Because of her above average intelligence such hostility will often take the form of sarcastic remarks and caustic comments. Despite the fact that she shows these aggressive responses she is not especially *assertive* and tends not to stick up for her rights unless strongly provoked. When this point is reached and she reacts strongly others may be surprised to see the change in an apparently quiet and submissive individual. Her emotional outbursts arouse guilt however and the aftermath of an aggressive scene will often be deep feelings of anxiety.

The best advice which one could give this girl would be to take an objective look at her current lifestyle and see if it is not possible to change things sufficiently to reduce current levels of stress. It would also be helpful for her to learn a more assertive approach to life, rather than relying on aggression when provoked. That is, she should stand up for herself from the start and safeguard her legitimate rights, rather than letting things slide to a point when an outburst of anger – and an attack on somebody else's rights – is the only outlet for her pent-up frustrations. She might also try to relax more and take things less seriously. This could help her through moments of crisis at work or in her private life.

We suggest that you now make use of this report, the information contained in the previous chapters and the Directory of the Hidden Language which starts on page 245 to prepare your own analysis of the second sample of handwriting.

Use the Funnel Method. Start by considering such overall features of the script as:

Appearance of the writing – is it released or rigid; does it have a forward or backward slope?

Pressure patterns – does it flow smoothly or show jerkiness and sudden upshoots?

Letter size – are the small letters similar in size or is there a considerable variability?

Relationship of capitals to ascenders – are they the same size, bigger or smaller?

Line straightness – has the writer managed to keep an even line or is there marked waviness?

When you have assessed these, and any other indications which seem significant, look at such specific aspects of the letter and word formation as:

Has the writer used anchor strokes?
Are the 'i' dots present or missing?
Do the 't' cross-strokes point downwards?
Is there any simplification of the script?
Are there scatter dots or pointed, downward dashes?

Examine the script carefully and extract as much information as possible. As you find different indications we suggest that you make a brief note of them. Once all the characteristics have been identified, begin to integrate them in order to produce a complete interpretation of the handwriting. Consider the likely influence of one indication over another. Is a particular symptom, perhaps of stress or physical weakness, confirmed or contradicted elsewhere in the text?

What kind of a personality would you expect the writer to possess? Draw up a Personality Profile and see if your interpretation of the eight major traits corresponds to ours.

What sort of health do you think the writer enjoys? How intelligent and educated do you take her to be? How you expect her to respond to a stressful situation?

All these and many more questions can be answered simply by carrying out an analysis of the handwriting sample shown below. Once you have arrived at conclusions about the writer, consider what advice you could offer. How does this writer differ in her approach to life to the young student whose script we have just looked at in so much detail? You can find out by comparing the Personality Profile which you have drawn up with the one we produced.

Handwriting Sample Two

The writer is a married woman aged 34 who works as an accounts director for a medium-sized chemical company. She has two daughters. That is all we are going to say about this subject. Now see what you can learn about her by analysing the sample of handwriting shown below:

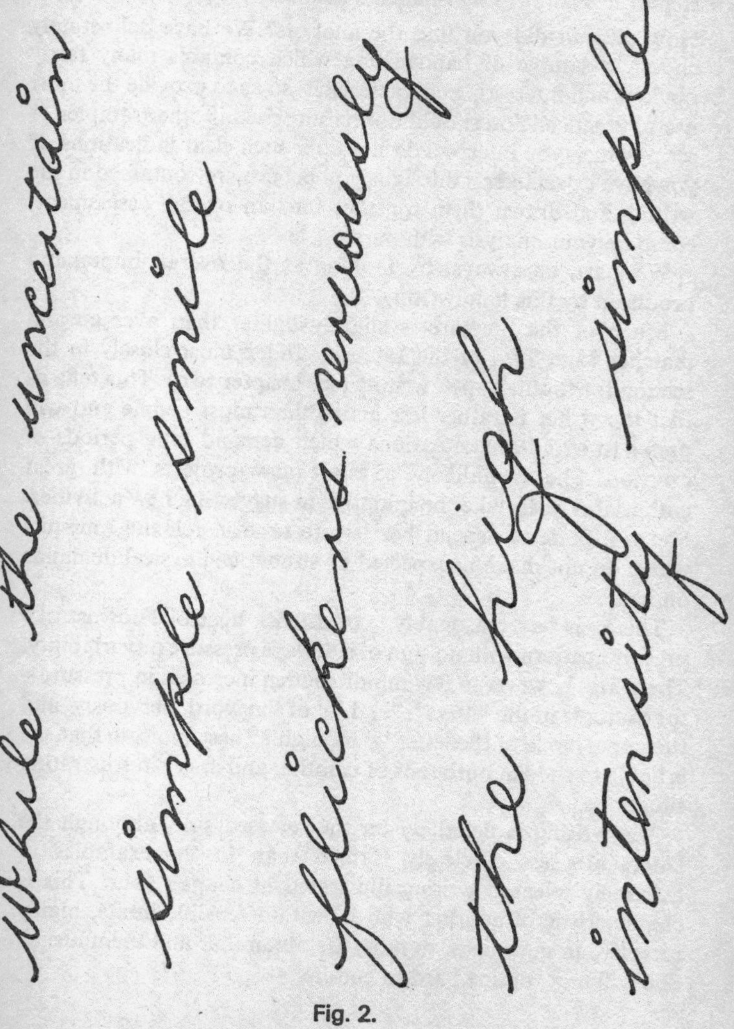

while the uncertain

simple smile

flickers nervously

the high simple

intensity of

Fig. 2.

When you have completed the analysis, read the analysis below to see how your interpretation compares with ours.

Report of Handwriting Sample Two

How difficult did you find the analysis? We have deliberately chosen a sample of handwriting which contains many fairly obvious and interesting characteristics so as to provide the most useful practice. You should not be surprised if other samples of script which you interpret do not offer such clear indications. If you have extracted all the signs you believe are contained in the writing and drawn them together into an overall assessment, compare your analysis with ours.

We start, as always, by looking at the overall impression produced by this handwriting.

Much of the pressure is slightly lighter than average and matches Line Two of the Intensity Index most closely in the section for fountain-pen writing (see chapter two). This tells us that the writer is rather less active than most people and will prefer to avoid any situations which demand long periods of exertion. She is unlikely to start new projects with great enthusiasm or to take the initiative in suggesting new activities. She will prefer to spend her leisure time in relaxing pursuits which do not make unexpected or strenuous physical demands on her.

There is a reasonably consistent upstroke-downstroke pressure pattern with no sign of sideways pressure or variability. There are, however, a few minor sudden increases in pressure – for example in the letters 'r' and 'u' of the word 'nervously' and the upper circle of the letter 'g' in 'high'. These indicate that she is liable to sudden outbursts of emotion and anger in frustrating situations.

The writing is definitely on the released side, although the letters are less carelessly formed than in the examples of extremely released writing illustrated in chapter four. This is characteristic of a writer who is, within sensible limits, highly receptive to new ideas, to fads, the unfamiliar and the unusual. She will find routine hard to endure.

The writing contains no artful simplifications and stays fairly close to the school-taught form. The only exceptions to this are the lower lengths in the letters 'g' and 'y', and the circle 'i' dots. These signs actually represent an *elaboration* rather than any attempt to simplify the writing and will be discussed in a moment. We can assume from this characteristic that she is of average or slightly above intelligence. (In a separate test this writer produced the speed test sentence described in chapter four in 12 seconds. This gives her a verbal ability in the top 10–15% of the population, which means she has an especially good facility with words and a deep understanding of written material.)

There is evidence of extraversion in the script, and the average rightwards slant of the letters gives her a score of two on this scale.

With the overall features of the writing considered, we can now focus in on specific aspects of the letter formation.

The first thing to notice is that the writer uses two types of starting strokes: *anchor strokes* (described in chapter one) and long, straight upstrokes which, we know from chapter six, are signs of aggression. Anchor strokes can be seen in the word 'while' at the start of the first line, the word 'flickers' in line three, and elsewhere. The long, straight upstrokes are present in the three different 's' letters at the start of words.

The anchor stroke tells us that the writer is rather dependent, lacking in confidence and passive. She will tend to conform to social pressures and the demands of conventional authority. She is very likely to hold fixed views and to resist logical arguments against them. When this sign is considered in relation to the signs of released writing discussed earlier, we can predict that she will be less likely than the average person to try and control her environment. This will make her very dependent on the demands of those around her and on events in her surroundings. She will not make sufficient effort to guide her own destiny and will tend to be tossed around at the whim of circumstances.

As we will see later in the analysis the anchor strokes point to characteristics which, when considered in relation to other tendencies indicated by the handwriting, suggest powerful conflicts in her personality and behaviour.

None of the 'i' dots are missing, which gives a score of zero on the independence scale.

When we consider the relationship between the height of capitals and ascenders we find that the only capital letter present, the 'W', of 'While', is approximately the same height as the ascenders (the 'h' and the 'l') in that word. This tells us that she is about average in assertiveness and would not be expected to be overly insistent on getting her own way or of giving in to the demands of others. Nevertheless, unless her wishes are not being directly opposed, she would not readily defer to the desires of others. This sign gives her a score of zero on these two dimensions of her personality.

Searching for any indications of Perfectionism we notice that the lines of the script are falling across the page. However, the large letter size and word spacing are such as almost to contradict this indication of perfectionism. We therefore give her a score of one, which indicates she is average on this trait and means she will not be over-concerned with details nor fussy about trivial matters. This sign, combined with her predominantly released writing flow, shows a considerable tolerance to the views, opinions and idiosyncracies of others. She will be equally understanding of ideas which are unusual or unconventional and can be expected to have a strong desire to express herself in original and nonconformist ways.

We must, however, also take into account her passivity and tendency to defer to the wishes of others which is likely to prevent her from fulfilling these inner needs. This conflict is likely to lead to some considerable frustration and dissatisfaction.

Two of the three 't' cross-strokes are curved slightly downwards (in the words 'the' of line four and 'intensity' of line five). This is not a very strong tendency, so we will only give her an Ambition Score of three. It suggests that the writer is somewhat above average on this personality trait and has a greater than normal need for achievement.

We will now consider the trait of Aggression for which there are several indications in the script. Notice, first of all, that she uses long, straight upstrokes on the first 's's of all three words which start with this letter. This gives a preliminary Aggression Score of two points. Then we find two clearly identifiable pointed dashes, one in the 't' of 'the' in line one and the other in the endstroke of the 's' in 'flickers' (line three). These mean an additional Aggression Score of one point. Finally, as we have already noticed, there are a few sudden, sharp increases in pressure which add another two points to the Aggression Score, a total of five marks. The score places her at the top end of the 'moderately aggressive' category and indicates that she will display open hostility on numerous occasions. We can expect her to give vent to sudden outbursts of temper and to row more often than most people.

This personality trait is in conflict with her need to defer to the wishes of others, with her dependency and her passivity. As a result she will exhibit see-saw behaviour, one moment quietly accepting the opinions and actions of others, no matter how frustrating she finds them, the next instant flying into a rage and lashing out furiously. It will be very hard to predict which of these very different responses is the most likely since it will depend on her mood at that moment.

We have already noted that the rightward slant to the script is sufficient to give her an Extraversion Score of two points. But there are specific signs of this trait within the letters as well which increase the total for this personality characteristic. Notice that the width of the small letters is, in most cases, as wide as or greater than the extreme width example given in chapter six. This is worth four points on the Extraversion Score. A further three points is awarded on the same scale because of the length of her lower extensions (i.e. on the 'g'; 'y'; and 'p's). This brings the total to nine which places her in the upper end of the 'Very Extraverted' category. We can say with confidence that she will be extremely expansive in her behaviour and have a strong need for the company of others. She will be gregarious, lively, blossom when in a social gathering, and dislike being alone. She will thrive on excitement and stimulation, tendencies likely to place her at risk, for example by driving too fast or taking unnecessary chances in order to get a thrill. She will become easily bored and long for constant variety and change in her life. She will readily express her feelings and, indeed, find it very hard to cover up her emotions and the influence which others have on her. As we explained in chapter six, people with a high score on the extroversion trait make pleasant companions but are often unreliable. Her total of nine means that she might be expected to miss appointments, turn up late on dates, forget promises or give assurances which are never followed through.

Another dominant trend in the handwriting which you might have spotted is sophistication. This is clearly shown by the circular 'i' dots – which give her a score of five points on this scale – and the embellishments which appear on about half the total number of lower loops present. These add three points to the score of Sophistication, making a total of eight. Such a score indicates that the writer has a strong desire to appear worldly and poised. Although extroverted and outgoing, she is somewhat emotionally detached from her frequent social encounters and may be superficial in personal relationships. She is probably manipulative and quick to exploit social contacts which have been developed by means of her extravert behaviour.

With this last trait considered we have obtained a handwriting score on each of the eight major aspects of personality and can now construct a Profile according to the method described in chapter six. Her scores were:

Independence	..	0
Assertiveness	..	0
Submissiveness	..	0
Perfectionism	..	0
Ambition	..	3
Aggression	..	5
Extraversion	..	9
Worldliness	..	8

When these scores have been drawn up in the form of a Profile we obtain the following:

Trait	Score				
	None	Mild	Moderate	Sub-stantial	Extreme
Independence	0	0	0	0	0
Assertiveness	0	0	0	0	0
Submissiveness	0	0	0	0	0
Perfectionism	0	0	0	0	0
Ambition	0	0	0	0	0
Aggression	0	0	0	0	0
Extraversion	0	0	0	0	0
Worldliness	0	0	0	0	0

The value of this method of drawing out the Personality Profile becomes clear if you now compare the completed chart for this writer with that of the student in this chapter or the male subject from chapter six. An immediate understanding of their overall personalities and the differences between them becomes possible. We can say how they will respond in different situations and how these responses will vary between each of the three subjects.

Such profiles are especially valuable if you are collecting information for some serious purposes, such as selecting applicants for a particular job or assessing the likely behaviour of individuals in different social situations.

Although the Personality Profile has been completed and we have managed to extract a fair amount of detailed information from those few lines of script, the task of interpretation is far from over. We noted that there were clear indications of aggression in the script as well as tendencies which are likely to result in conflict and frustrations which will probably be expressed in either a highly passive or extremely emotional way.

It will be useful, therefore, to see what other information about the writer's emotional make-up can be discerned from the sample.

The ink colour was blue-black so we cannot find any clues there. No isolated ambiguity or fractured words are present in the script. Are there any indications at all of emotional disturbance? One of the most obvious signs is the variability of the small letters. Notice the difference in size between the letters in the word 'nervously', and compare the height of the words 'the high' (line four) with those at the start of the script. A more detailed examination brings to light indications of stroke jerk. Look, for instance, at the letter 'h' in line four.

As these are the only indications of emotional disturbance we can conclude that, although she is likely to be somewhat more emotional than most and at times over-react, the writer is able to control her feelings and not allow them to create any major problems in her life. There are no signs of emotional constipation and, indeed, many indications that she expresses herself freely and does not try to cover up her feelings.

One major sign of compulsivity is present and we wonder if you spotted it? This is contained in the upper extension of the letter 'h' in the word. This has a loop which the writer added on after completing the letter (the indication becomes more obvious if you use a magnifying glass). This tells us that she will react to anxiety by some form of repetitious behaviour, the psychological 'undoing' which was described in chapter seven. Although not a major characteristic of her script it is sufficiently well indicated to suggest that, despite her below average activity level, she may strive to complete any task which causes anxiety by repeating the same response over and over again.

Finally, did you notice the number of resting dots present in the script? These occur mostly at the start of words where the writer has paused momentarily before continuing with the effort of writing. Resting dots can clearly be seen in the 'w' of 'while' (line one) and the 's' in 'simple' (line two). This shows that she is experiencing some exhaustion, although this is not severe. It may be due to stress or even a temporary state of tiredness. Finally, no signs of mental or physical ill-health are present.

We hope that you were able to spot at least some of the main characteristics described in our report. If you overlooked a few, we suggest that you study the sample again and make certain that you can identify all the key signs in the handwriting. Remember that you should strive to integrate both the small indications of the writer's health, personality and emotional state with the overall picture presented by the script. Identifying the important characteristics and then developing an overall assessment which is accurate and reliable takes practice. If you only spotted one or two of the characteristics in the examples given in this chapter do not feel too depressed or assume that carrying out a successful analysis is an especially complex task. It is only a matter of training your eye to notice points of importance and of training your brain to associate all the indications within the script so that a meaningful story can be told and reliable predictions developed. We suggest that you start out by looking at the handwriting of family and friends, where you know the people well enough to be able to confirm your judgements based on the script from personal knowledge. But while doing so watch out for one major danger which could seriously bias the results. Never let what knowledge you have of the writer, or believe that you have, colour your assessment. It is all too easy to read into the script signs which you feel *should* be there from what you already know about the individual. This can lead to serious errors. Very often it is actually easier to analyse the handwriting of a complete stranger because of this problem. The advantage of starting with those well known to you is simply that, if you are uncertain about a judgement, you can usually ask for advice from them as to whether or not they feel it to be a valid assessment.

One frequent response from subjects, once you have become proficient in graphonomy, is astonishment! Complete surprise that you have been able to learn so much about them, so rapidly and from such seemingly trivial evidence as a few casually written words. That such revelations are the inevitable outcome of the penetrating techniques of this astonishing new science should no longer come as any surprise to you.

Graphonomy provides the passport for the start of a fascinating voyage of human discovery. Not only can those who have mastered its procedures gain a greater knowledge and understanding of others but, no less rewardingly, it may be used to acquire deep and invaluable self-insights.

Nearly two hundred years ago the Scots poet Robert Burns made a passionate plea for those very skills when he wrote:

> 'Oh would some power the giftie gie us,
> To see ourselves as others see us!
> It would from many a blunder free us,
> An' foolish notion.'

This is the remarkable promise made by graphonomy. This is the exciting power offered to those who have learned to read the secret story of a person's script and to properly interpret the hidden language of handwriting.

Dictionary of Graphonomy

This dictionary has been laid out on the basis of the Funnel Method of analysis described in chapter two. Overall indications to look out for are presented first and then more specific features of the letter formation are listed in alphabetical order.

Overall Indications

Description	Interpretation	See Page
Artfully simplified writing	High general intelligence.	73
Columning (In children) (In adults)	Over-concern with need for order. Feelings of insecurity. A disturbed personality.	218
Crowded words	Perfectionist mentality.	130
Falling lines	Perfectionist mentality.	129
Heavy crossing out of errors	Anxiety over mistakes, fears of incompetence.	202
Illegibility – extreme (In children)	Emotionally disturbed.	199

Overall Indications

Description	Interpretation	See Page
Illegibility – uncontrolled (In children)	Impulsive, poor motor skills.	204
Originality of style (In children)	Independent. Early development. Above average intelligence.	206
Ineffective word alignment (In children)	Poorly developed attentional skills.	213
Pressure heavy	Active, energetic, able to exert intense effort.	42
Pressure, increases suddenly	Quick temper, aggressive.	62
Pressure light	Lacking in energy, displays minimal activity.	54
Pressure random	Nervous, anxious, prone to emotional upsets.	61
Released writing	Readily expresses emotions, impulsive, superficial, happy-go-lucky.	82
Restrained writing	Cautious, strives to maintain control.	82
Rigid, angular	Directly or indirectly expressed aggression.	203

Overall Indications

Description	Interpretation	See Page
Slant – backwards	Emotional disturbance.	155
Slant – forwards	Extrovert personality, sociable and outgoing.	138
Slant – variability	Emotional disturbance.	155
Small writing	Perfectionist mentality.	129
Uncontrolled illegibility (In children)	Impulsive, poor co-ordination.	204
Unnecessary writing	Anxious striving, sensitivity to criticism.	203
Wavy writing lines (In children) (In adults)	Problems of attending. Emotional disturbance.	212 158
Large signature	High self-esteem or imagined self-importance.	98
Small signature	Avoids limelight, dislikes acclaim, low self-esteem.	99
Initial instead of first name	Socially conservative, little self-disclosure.	111
First name used	More than averagely liberal, above average self-disclosure.	111

Overall Indications

Description	Interpretation	See Page
Scrawled signature	Feelings of self-importance.	115
Underlined signature	Self-confident, exhuberant, enthusiastic.	116
Overly decorated signature	Outwardly conventional but desire to be non-conformist.	117

Specific Indications within letter strokes

Description	Interpretation	See Page
Anchor strokes	Conformist; somewhat immature emotionally; accepts views of authority; ambitious within a conventional framework of behaviour.	20
Bizarre letter forms	Sign of mental illness.	194
Blurring and blotching	As above.	194
Broken upper loops	Emotional disturbance.	160
Capitals larger than ascenders	Assertive, outspoken, resistant to persuasion.	125

Specific Indications within letter strokes

Description	Interpretation	See Page
Capitals smaller than ascenders	Submissive, passive, yield to desires of others.	125
Childlike script (In adults)	Mental illness.	192
Circular 'i' dots	Attempt to convey air of sophistication, desire to be regarded as socially aware. In teenagers often a sign of a desire for independence.	142
Cross-stroke pressure	Over-striving, high need for achievement, sacrifices personal life for attainment of goals.	57
Curtailment	Emotional restraint.	163
Downward 't' bar	High need for achievement, very ambitious.	132
End of word pressure	Aggressive personality.	135
Extreme writing line disturbance	Mental illness.	193
Fading	Excessive stress.	172
Fractured words	Have emotional significance for the writer.	151

Specific Indications within letter strokes

Description	Interpretation	See Page
Increased height and height variability	After drinking. Writer is intoxicated.	178
Increased width and width variability	After drinking. Writer is intoxicated.	178
Ink trails	Physical weakness.	188
Isolated ambiguity	Concern for concealment.	152
Letter distortion	Mental illness.	192
Letter lurches	Sign of compulsiveness.	174
Letter splitting	Mental illness.	194
Letter stutter	Sign of compulsiveness.	166
Line overlap	Emotional disturbance.	157
Long lower extensions	Extravert personality, sociable and outgoing.	138
Lower loop embellishment	Desire to be seen as worldly and sophisticated. In teenagers indicates a quest for independence.	142
Missing 'i' dots	Independent; non-conformist; Self-sufficient.	122

Specific Indications within letter strokes

Description	Interpretation	See Page
Long, straight upstrokes	Aggression.	135
Narrow upper loops	Emotional disturbance.	157
Overwriting	Compulsiveness.	167
Poorly co-ordinated writing	Emotional disturbance.	158
Pointed downward dashes	Aggression.	134
Resting dots	Stress problem.	173
Scatter dots	Physical weakness.	188
Segmentation	As above.	187
Stroke jerks	Emotional disturbance.	159
Stroke tacking	Physical weakness.	188
Sudden upshoot	Associated with lung diseases.	188

Additional Indications

Colour of inks used. Only applies when these colours are chosen habitually and from choice (see pages 148-151).

Green Ink	Otherwise suppressed desire to be different, nonconformist and original. Can indicate an emotional disturbance.
Red Ink	A disturbed personality.
Black Ink	An over-concern with precision in communications. A desire to be clearly understood.

References

CHAPTER 1

Allport, G. W. and Vernon, P. E. (1933) *Studies in Expressive Movement*. NY: Macmillan.

Lemke, E. A. and Kirchner, J. H. (1971) A multivariate study of handwriting, intelligence, and personality correlates. *Journal of Personality Assessment*, 35: 585–593.

Linton, H. B., Epstein, L., and Hartford, H. (1961) Personality and perceptual correlates of secondary beginning strokes in handwriting. *Perceptual and Motor Skills*, 12: 271–281.

Pearl, R. (1974) *The Value of Handwriting in the Neurologic Examination*. Mount Sinai Journal of Medicine, 41: 200–204.

Sonnemann, U. (1950) *Handwriting Analysis as a Psychodiagnostic Tool*. NY: Grune and Stratton.

Wieser, R. (1956) *Der Verbrecher und seine Handschrift*. (The Criminal and His Handwriting) Munich: Reinhardt.

CHAPTER 3

Pascal, G. (1943) Handwriting pressure: Its measurement and significance. *Character and Personality*, 11: 235–254.

CHAPTER 4

Binet, A. (1906) *Les Revelations de l'Ecriture d'apres un Controle Scientifique*. Paris: Alcan.

Castelnuovo-Tedesco, P. (1948) A study of the relationship between handwriting and personality variables. *Genetic Psychology Monographs*, 37: 167–220.

Cattell, R. B. and Warburton, F. W. *Objective Personality and Motivation Tests*. Urbana, Ill.: University of Illinois Press, 1969.

Epstein, L., Hartfore, H., and Tumarkin, I. (1961) The relationship of certain letter form variants in the handwriting of female subjects to their education, intelligence, and age. *Journal of Experimental Education*, 29: 385–392.

Pophal, R. (1950) Das Strichbild: *Zum Form und Stoffproblem in der Psychologie der Handschrift*. Stuttgart: Thieme.

CHAPTER 5

Boshier, R. (1973) Name style and conservatism. *Journal of Psychology*, 84: 45–53.

Zweigenhaft, R. L. and Marlow, D. (1973) Signature size: Studies in expressive movement. *Journal of Consulting and Clinical Psychology*, 40: 469–473.

CHAPTER 6

Eysenck, J. J. (1967) *The Biological Basis of Personality*. Springfield, Ill.: Thomas.

Harvey, O. L. (1934) The measurement of handwriting considered as a form of expressive movement. *Character and Personality*, 2: 310–321.

Loewenthal, K. (1975) Handwriting and self-presentation. *Journal of Social Psychology*, 96: 267–270.

McNeil, E. and Blum, G. (1952) Handwriting and psychosexual dimensions of personality. *Journal of Projective Techniques*, 16: 476–484.

Williams, M., Berg-Cross, C., and Berg-Cross, L. (1977) Handwriting characteristics and their relationship to Eysenck's extroversion-introversion, and Kagan's impulsivity-reflectivity dimensions. *Journal of Personality Assessment*, 41: 291–298.

CHAPTER 7

Rottersman, W. (1944) *Journal of Nervous and Mental Disorders*, 100: 507–510.

CHAPTER 8

Brun, B. and Riesby, W. (1971) Handwriting changes following meprobamate and alcohol. *Quarterly Journal of Studies in Alcohol*, 32: 1070–1082.

Douglas, D. B. and Sara, D. (1975) Handwriting in schizophrenia: Some clinical observations. *Diseases of the Nervous System*, 36: 561–567.

Haase, H. J., Floru, L., and Knack, M. (1974) The clinical importance of the neuroleptic threshold and its fine motor determinants. *Journal of International Medical Research*, 2: 321–330.

Kanfer, A. and Casten, P. F. (1958) Observation on disturbances in neuromuscular co-ordination in patients with malignant disease. *Bulletin of the Hospital of Joint Diseases*, 19: 1–19.

Tripp, C. A., Fluckiger, F. A., and Weinberg, G. H. (1959) Effects of alcohol on the graphomotor performances of normals and alcoholics. *Perceptual and Motor Skills*, 9: 227–236.

CHAPTER 9

Chapman, L. J. and Wendell, K. (1972) Perceptual-motor abilities and reversal errors in children's handwriting. *Journal of Learning Disorders*, 5: 321–325.
Oinen, P. (1960) Huono kasiala psykilogisema onglemana. (Poor handwriting as a psychological problem.) *Acta Academiae Paedagogicae Jyvaskylaensis*, 21: 163–170.
Roman, C. (1968) *Encyclopedia of the Written Word*. NY: F. Ungar.
Soloff, S. (1973) The effect of non-content factors on the grading of essays. *Graduate Research in Education and Related Disciplines*, 6: 44–54.

Fiction

☐	**The Island**	Peter Benchley	£1.25p
☐	**Options**	Freda Bright	£1.50p
☐	**Dupe**	Liza Cody	£1.25p
☐	**Chances**	Jackie Collins	£2.25p
☐	**Brain**	Robin Cook	£1.75p
☐	**The Entity**	Frank De Felitta	£1.75p
☐	**Whip Hand**	Dick Francis	£1.50p
☐	**Secrets**	Unity Hall	£1.50p
☐	**Solo**	Jack Higgins	£1.75p
☐	**The Rich are Different**	Susan Howatch	£2.75p
☐	**The Master Sniper**	Stephen Hunter	£1.50p
☐	**Moviola**	Garson Kanin	£1.50p
☐	**The Master Mariner**		
	Book 1: Running Proud	Nicholas Monsarrat	£1.50p
☐	**Platinum Logic**	Tony Parsons	£1.75p
☐	**Fools Die**	Mario Puzo	£1.50p
☐	**The Boys in the Mailroom**	Iris Rainer	£1.50p
☐	**A Married Man**	Piers Paul Read	£1.50p
☐	**Sunflower**	Marilyn Sharp	95p
☐	**The Throwback**	Tom Sharpe	£1.50p
☐	**Wild Justice**	Wilbur Smith	£1.75p
☐	**That Old Gang of Mine**	Leslie Thomas	£1.25p
☐	**Caldo Largo**	Earl Thompson	£1.50p
☐	**Ben Retallick**	E. V. Thompson	£1.75p

All these books are available at your local bookshop or newsagent, or
can be ordered direct from the publisher. Indicate the number of copies
required and fill in the form below

Name_____
(Block letters please)

Address_____

_____

Send to Pan Books (CS Department), Cavaye Place, London SW10 9PG
Please enclose remittance to the value of the cover price plus:
35p for the first book plus 15p per copy for each additional book ordered
to a maximum charge of £1.25 to cover postage and packing
Applicable only in the UK

While every effort is made to keep prices low, it is sometimes
necessary to increase prices at short notice. Pan Books reserve
the right to show on covers and charge new retail prices which
may differ from those advertised in the text or elsewhere